ON THE LINE

LIFE ON THE US-MEXICAN BORDER

AUGUSTA DWYER

LAB

Acknowledgements

The author would like to thank the following for their help and cooperation in the realisation of this book:

Ed Kreuger, Julia Quiñones, Cristina Hernández, Willivaldo Delgadillo, Debbie Nathan, Dick Kamp, Phil Gasper, Joe Allen, Carmen Valades, Jaime Cota, Gloria de la O, Adriana Nolasco.

Research from this book was made possible by a grant from The Canada Council.

The Latin America Bureau is an independent research and publishing organisation. It works to broaden public understanding of issues of human rights and social and economic justice in Latin America and the Caribbean.

First published in the UK in 1994 by the Latin America Bureau (Research and Action) Ltd, 1 Amwell Street, London EC1R 1UL

A CIP catalogue record for this book is available from the British Library

ISBN 0 906156 84 X (pbk)

Editor: Duncan Green
Cover design: Andy Dark
Map: Tim Aspden, Dept. of Geography, UCL

Printed by Russell Press, Nottingham NG7 3HN
Trade distribution in UK by Central Books, 99 Wallis Road, London E9 5LN
Distribution in North America by Monthly Review Press, 122 West 27th Street, New York, NY 10001

Contents

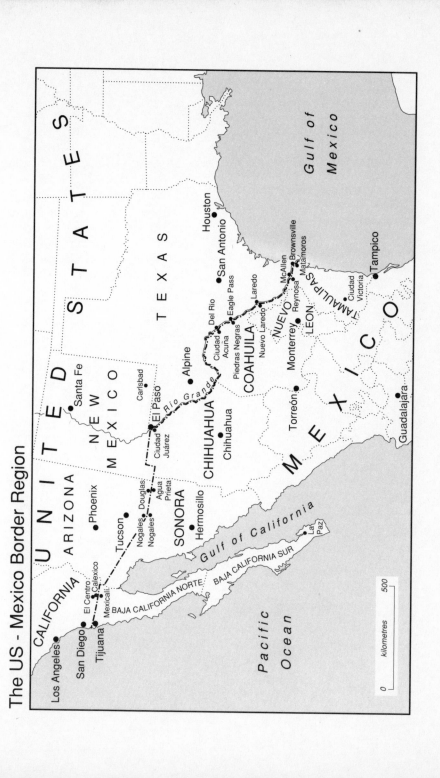

The US - Mexico Border Region

Preface

At first glance, the borderlands between Mexico and the United States may seem an odd place in which to spend time, let alone write about. Lost between the two nations, they offer little to excite the visitor in the way of culture, politics or even nature. The temperatures are extremely uncomfortable, and no town or city I visited there could be described as charming or picturesque. 'Underwhelming', I noted in my journal of my first trip across the Rio Grande, during an inaugural visit to El Paso, Texas in 1991, 'not so much a river but a pair of cemented-in canals at this point. I caught an old bus with bright red seats across the Santa Fe bridge after a long wait in front of the Paisano Five and Dime. A few homeless men drifted past me, their skin sunburnt and their hair stiff with street grime.'

While its sheer length - 2,000 miles - makes any kind of pat, one-phrase summary impossible, all my journeys revealed a cross-border panorama of poverty and venality set in a desert landscape. Yet behind the tough, unpromising exterior, I found inspiring people embroiled in some fascinating issues. For me, the border raised at least three important questions, which I decided to explore in this book: What happens when a wealthy nation moves hundreds of its factories to a much poorer country next door? Furthermore, what happens to the dusty, half-forgotten, mostly rural towns when they are sucked overnight into the industrial world? Finally, what happens when hundreds of thousands of migrants from the poor nation illegally cross the border and find jobs in the wealthy neighbour's economy, one which faces growing strains in its own economic and political situation? These issues hit me hardest when I arrived in Tijuana for the first time, and was brought to a halt by the swirling crowds on a wide shopping street, its sidewalks packed with vendors and shoppers, tourists and would-be emigrants from all over Mexico.

The issues raised in this book have taken on greater significance as time goes on. The question of illegal immigration in the United States is now a decidedly hot one, with politicians linking the presence of Latino immigrants to crime and high taxes, despite the evidence that they are in fact a boon to the US economy.

Meanwhile, controversy surrounds the implementation of the North American Free Trade Agreement, which passed through the stages of negotiation, signing and finally ratification in the US Congress while this book was being researched and written. Throughout the process, heated arguments revolved around the *maquiladora* assembly plants strung along the Mexican-US border. The reaction to NAFTA has grown from a nationalist, our-jobs-first mentality among some small groups to a much wider movement of solidarity among workers of the three nations, resulting in a 50,000-strong anti-NAFTA demonstration in Ottawa, Canada in July 1993 and an intense lobbying effort in the US before the fateful Congressional vote in November 1993. More recently, the condemnation of NAFTA has even been taken up by indigenous insurgents in Mexico's poorest southern state, Chiapas.

The free trade agreement clearly shows the importance of Mexico to US and Canadian business, a trend confirmed by Mexico's recent entry to the 'Rich Men's Club' of the Organisation for Economic Co-operation and Development (OECD). As Mexico wins accolades from international investors and businessmen, its other side must also be investigated and exposed - the Mexico where democracy is in short supply, living standards are appalling, wages rock-bottom and working conditions inhumane.

In the end, what the US-Mexican border reveals, and what this book tries to show, is that the greatest border between peoples is not between nations, but between those who wield power and those who must suffer the consequences.

Augusta Dwyer, Mexico City, May 1994

1
Petra

Welcome to the Border

It happened during the night shift at General Electric's modern Sociedad de Motores plant in Reynosa, at the end of a hot August day in 1991.

The shift began at 8.30pm. At around eight, Petra Santiago left her yellow plywood shack in Colonia Roma, crossed the narrow wooden planks over the drainage trench and, picking her way through the mesquite bushes and rubbish and mud, climbed the roadside ditch to the Monterrey highway. Waving her hand, she stopped a bus that would take her to work, just a few kilometres down the road to the Reynosa Industrial Park.

At the time, Petra was four months pregnant with her third child. She wasn't married to the child's father, Oscar Figueroa, but they had a steady relationship. She also looked after her two children from a previous marriage.

By law, pregnant women are not allowed to work night shifts in Mexico. The company is supposed to assign them day shifts and allow them an extra half hour rest period. But by mid-1991 Petra had been assembling and quality-checking motors for GE air conditioners for three years. She was already accustomed to the big American company's lack of attention to these matters, just as she was used to the obligatory overtime, the nine-and-a-half-hour shifts and the lousy pay of US$38 per week.

At around 10.30 that night, two hours after her shift began, Petra suddenly felt sharp pains in her abdomen. She left the brightly-lit quality control area to find that night's supervisor, Martín Ríos, and told him that she needed to go to the local hospital. All *maquiladora* workers like Petra are insured for medical benefits at the state-run hospitals of the Mexican Institute of Social Security (IMSS). But they are also prevented, under threat of immediate and automatic dismissal, from leaving the factory floor during their shifts without management permission. Ríos fobbed Petra off. 'Just go and see the duty nurse,' he told her, and in spite of her misgivings, Petra went.

The nurse gave her a couple of aspirins. 'She told me to take one right then and the other eight hours later and that would take care of the pain,' says Petra. 'But I knew they wouldn't work. And besides, I've always heard that when you're pregnant you shouldn't take any kind of drugs. So I went on feeling sick until, at one in the morning, I asked the supervisor a second time if I could go and see a doctor at the IMSS.'

Again Ríos said no. Hadn't she already been to see the nurse, he asked with irritation. Petra told him that the nurse had just given her an aspirin, but the pain was so bad that she could hardly walk. Ríos said she must be faking.

'The third time,' Petra recalls, 'was around 3am. I spoke to the line foreman and he said, "Look, if you're that sick, go." I spoke to the supervisor again and he still wouldn't let me leave. I kept on working until about a quarter to six, and that's when I started to haemorrhage, right there on the factory floor.'

Petra's younger sister Candi, who worked on the assembly line making coils, ran to get the nurse while two other women helped Petra to the women's washroom. There the nurse found her and gave her two sanitary towels. 'Here, put these on,' she told Petra, adding, 'Oh, and I guess you'd better go to hospital.'

❈   ❈   ❈   ❈   ❈

One year later Petra can talk about it all in a pretty matter-of-fact tone of voice, sounding indignant, mostly. She has had another child with Oscar since, and standing there rocking the tiny, sickly-looking infant, she seems older than her 25 years. In a faded black T-shirt and black shorts, straight brown hair clipped short and dark eyes slightly narrowed, she wears a knowing, almost cynical air like a shield, the typical show of resilience of a poor yet proud Mexican woman who must take her hard life for granted to survive. She still lives in the yellow plywood shack, which still has no running water or bathroom or basic comforts of any kind. Outside she has hung some tin cans of flowers from the roof, but nothing can mask its most outstanding characteristic - squalor.

The tiny yard is enclosed by old wooden pallets. It is dry and weedy except for a stunted acacia tree growing in one corner. A few chickens wander around and a small pig lives trapped inside a crude wooden pen. The door to the latrine is off its hinges, and has to be yanked into place and left leaning everytime someone needs to use it. A mysterious long board, upholstered with odd bits of coloured cloth, leans against the corrugated metal roof like a ladder.

All of Colonia Roma looks like this. A rubbish-filled hollow, spreading out beyond a busy spot on the Reynosa - Monterrey highway, it is known as a place where migrant workers on their way to Texas stop off for a few days or weeks before attempting the illegal crossing of the Río Grande. *Paracaidistas*, people call them, parachutists. They drop in, then go. Open trenches have been dug to carry away waste water and here and there, narrow makeshift bridges cross them to join mud paths through the brush to the desperate, ugly homes. All summer long the place is pervaded by the smell of rubbish in the over-a-hundred-degree heat. Rubbish, mud, the contents of the jerry-built latrines; it is as if the whole place is rotting.

Worst of all, every time it rains, the hollow fills with water, sending the discarded flotsam of poverty - ragged clothes, half-empty plastic containers of food, a dirty plush toy animal - floating up and out of the abandoned shacks, to form a permanent dump in a wide rim right in front of the shanty town. 'The last time it rained, the water came right up to here,' says Petra, indicating a place on the kitchen wall about waist height.'

The heat inside Petra's house at noon is almost indescribable. A cockroach the size of a small mouse clambers over the uneven, packed-earth floor. Racks of plastic dishes are nailed to the wall and a pot of beans boils on the gas stove. A calendar and a few magazine pages flap from the wall. Through a narrow wooden door is the shack's second room, dark, mattresses and bedding on the floor, wrinkled clothes hanging from nails on the wall.

Petra's older sister Mary is sitting in the kitchen with us. She lives in a shack - this one pink - just beside Petra's, with her husband, Martín, and three children; Candi and her husband and two children have a blue shack on the other side. Both Martín and Candi still work for GE. While we're talking, Candi comes in to say good-bye, then leaves for the afternoon shift at Sociedad de Motores. Her youngest child, two-year-old Joaquín, frets when she goes, leaving Mary to calm him down as well as cope with her own one-year-old.

The Santiago Dávila sisters were never meant to live like this, if indeed anyone is ever meant to. Originally from Poza Rica, in the state of Veracruz, their family used to be fairly well-off, owning a string of snack stands. 'We sold fruit drinks, pop, tacos, things like that,' explains Mary, recounting the family history. 'I remember every three weeks we'd go to the Central Market in Mexico City and buy everything we needed for all the stands. It was a good business.'

Then the sisters' mother died and their father took to drink. Before long the stands had all been sold and the family's money gone. Petra was the first one, in 1988, to head up to the border town of Reynosa, just across the Río Grande from Texas' Hidalgo County and the cities of McAllen and Edinburg.

The sisters had an aunt living in Reynosa who had written to say that jobs were plentiful there. Since her husband had just left her with two small children to look after, Petra thought that a *maquila* job might be the solution to her problems. A year later, Candi and Mary and their families joined her. They've been living in the poverty of Colonia Roma ever since.

❋   ❋   ❋   ❋   ❋

Colonia Roma is typical of the living conditions of *maquiladora* workers and the low wages that characterise the industry. Those wages - a fraction of what workers in the United States and Canada earn - are the bottom line advantage to setting up a *maquiladora* on the Mexican border.

American Chamber of Commerce estimates for 1992 show *maquiladora* wages ranging from a low of .57 cents an hour in Torreón to US$1.95 in Matamoros. The average for the *maquiladora* industry throughout Mexico barely exceeds one dollar an hour.

Yet even though wages are so low, prices are often higher than in the US and *maquiladora* workers frequently cross the border to shop, bringing a large percentage of their wages back to the US economy. In Hidalgo County, *maquila* employees add over US$9 million to the economy; in Del Río, Texas, across the river from Ciudad Acuña, shoppers spent US$10.5 million in 1989, according to Chamber of Commerce estimates. In El Paso, retail sales to Mexican shoppers now add one billion dollars a year to the local economy, according to that city's Chamber of Commerce.

Small-time vendors can buy goods across the river, sell them at double the price back on the Mexican side and still undercut Mexican shopkeepers. Business fell drastically in American border towns and riots broke out in Nuevo Laredo in late 1992 when the Mexican government announced a new law reducing the value of duty-free goods people could bring back across the border from US$300 to US$50. When the Mexican currency was devalued in 1982, days after then-president José López Portillo had said he 'would defend the peso like a dog,' a large number of shops in American cities like Brownsville and El Paso went out of business as Mexican shoppers suddenly found US prices impossibly high.

Just as the *maquiladoras* cluster along the southern side of the border, second-hand clothing stores dot the American side, selling cast-offs by the pound rather than by item. Enterprising Mexicans cross the border regularly to purchase large bundles or *pacas*, of bound clothing, displaying them along fences or under trees in poor Mexican *colonias* from the Gulf of Mexico to the Pacific. As one woman *maquila* worker in Tijuana puts it, when asked how she copes with such low wages, 'Well, you don't really. It barely gives you enough for food. I just say thank God that even though they're second-hand from the States, you can still buy clothes.'

Transport to and from work in the industrial parks which house the *maquiladoras* is usually chaotic and expensive. Some companies provide old school buses, but in cities like Reynosa or nearby Matamoros, workers, students and shoppers alike must crowd into tiny, converted vans, paying 30 cents a trip. Anyone with an inside line to either the mayor or the local pro-government union can set up a bus service, providing uncomfortable transport devoid of safety and anti-polluting measures.

Ever since *maquiladoras* became popular with American and other foreign business, suburbs of shacks began spreading all along *la frontera*, reaching further and further beyond the border cities' limits. Crowded, dirty, and dusty, they transform the varied northern landscapes into scenes of unalloyed misery. Few homes have running water, sanitary drainage or electricity. In winter they are freezing and in summer, stiflingly hot. Mothers who work on the assembly lines often have no choice but to leave their children at home to look after themselves and they often turn to drugs or gang violence as they grow older.

Open ditches run with human and toxic industrial wastes, while only the most progressive of municipal authorities will admit that because the foreign companies pay no local taxes, they have no money to provide services for the thousands of new residents flooding into their cities every year. The air swirls with the residues of burning plastics and chemicals, as well as faecal dust picked up by the wind from the inadequate drainage trenches in the poor *colonias*. Respiratory problems are becoming increasingly common and the environmental degradation quickly spreads. River water containing factory run-off is used to irrigate crops and pasture, potentially contaminating food that is eaten throughout Mexico and even exported. Gas or chemical leaks in Mexican towns float across the border to their American neighbours.

Health and safety violations abound in the myriad Fortune 500[1] factories that cluster at or near the border. Mexican law absolves foreign companies from legal suits for work-related accidents, confining awards to a government-set minimum, thus relieving corporations of the kinds of hefty payments for which they might be liable in the US or Canada. Instead, injuries are summarily dealt with by evermore strained state health and pension budgets. All kinds of unfair labour practices - everything from firing workers for trying to organise to firing those who have earned seniority and reasonable severance payments - are common. So is the sexual harassment of female workers, hiring minors, and closing up and leaving town without bothering to pay the final week's wages or severance pay.

❋ ❋ ❋ ❋ ❋

Mexico now has more than 2,180 *maquiladoras* throughout the country. They are also known as in-bond plants, because their components enter Mexico temporarily without duty, or 'in bond' for assembly. To offset the image of *maquiladoras* as runaway plants, avoiding US wages and health and safety standards, they are also referred to as twin plants, a name which suggests a manufacturing process involving both US and Mexican plants working in partnership. The *maquiladoras*, however, are more often paired with warehouses or offices across the border, than factories.

According to the country's National Institute of Geography and Statistics (INEGI), 83 per cent of the *maquiladoras* are spread along Mexico's 2,000-mile-long border with the US, employing almost 86 per cent of the total workforce. Some companies favour big cities like Matamoros at the mouth of the Río Grande, across from Brownsville, Texas, or Ciudad Juárez, across from El Paso, or Tijuana, across the land border from San Diego, California. But the ever-growing need for labour has also forced them to set up in small towns, barely locatable on a map before the *maquila* boom, such as Piedras Negras and Ciudad Acuña, across the river from Eagle Pass and Del Río, Texas, respectively, or Agua Prieta and Nogales, neighbouring Douglas and Nogales, both in Arizona. *Maquiladoras* are now springing up in central cities such as Guadalajara, and can be found as far south as the Yucatán.

The *maquiladora* programme, also known as the Border Industrialization Programme, is based on the quick assembly in Mexico of parts and raw materials from either the US or other countries. The word *maquiladora* comes from the share of grain a miller would keep in payment for milling grain during colonial times in Mexico, and refers to the idea of a single step in a longer process going on elsewhere.

Mexico's Trade Secretariat (SECOFI) defines a *maquiladora* as any plant where the machinery and raw materials are 'temporarily imported', only to be assembled and shipped back out again. Companies are exempt from the 2 per cent assets tax charged everywhere else in Mexico, paying only a small tax on the value added to the product. Both American and other companies have a further advantage that their assembled product can come back into the US duty free, thanks to a 1962 US Customs regulation.

The *maquiladoras* in northern Mexico now assemble almost every imaginable item in use in modern society - from car parts, clothing, and electrical appliances to hospital materials, furniture and computer parts. Even missile components for the US Department of Defense are assembled in Circuitos Binacionales de Tijuana, a *maquila* belonging to Hughes Aircraft Co., a subsidiary of General Motors.

Collectively these plants are part of an industrial process known as globalisation, whereby manufacturing has been broken down into a thousand tiny steps, each worker at times spending no more than a few minutes on each part of the production process, and those workers are spread out all over the world. This kind of off-shore manufacturing plays an increasing role in keeping hundreds of American companies, and by extension a fair section of the American economy, afloat.

Service industries, such as entering data into computers, are also becoming popular. A close look at the fine print on any coupon offering discounts on all kinds of Canadian and US products, for example, almost invariably instructs merchants to redeem costs by sending them to places like Del Río or El Paso. Across the river legions of young women are sorting and entering numbers for companies such as Carolina Coupon Processing, Seven Oaks, and A.C. Nielson, which buy the coupons from merchants for the discount price and then get the money back from the various manufacturers.

Over half a million Mexicans now work in this vast chain of plants and workshops, according to INEGI, a figure that currently fluctuates between 14 and 16 per cent of the country's entire manufacturing sector employment. In terms of output and exports, the *maquiladoras* easily constitute the fastest growing sector in industry in Mexico. The number of plants increased at a rate of over nine per cent in 1992, and at 4.7 per cent for the first ten months of 1993, down from the 16 per cent annual growth rate registered between 1983 and 1990 due to the knock-on effect of the US recession. Over the first three quarters of 1993, however, the value of *maquila* exports grew by 17.6 per cent compared to the same period in 1992, according to the Bank of Mexico, reaching US$15.6 billion. By October 1993, employment in the *maquila* industry had grown by 7.2 per cent over the first ten months of the previous year.

Most of the *maquiladoras*, 68 per cent according to 1991 American Chamber of Commerce statistics, are wholly owned by US firms. Another 25 per cent of total investment comes from Mexican entrepreneurs, most of whom work with an exclusive contract to supply assembled parts to a US company. Japanese investment increased greatly in the late 1980s, but still only represents 4 per cent, There are now 50 Japanese-owned *maquilas*, mostly based in Tijuana and Mexicali in Baja California state, compared to just five in 1985. The remainder of the investment comes from small numbers of European, Canadian and Korean companies.

The reason so many foreign companies, especially from the US, move their plants to Mexico is simple. They are close to American markets and transport costs are minimal. The Mexican workforce is young, hard-working, literate, and skilful. Unions are practically non-existent, or where they do exist, pliant to the wishes of either *maquiladora* owners or the ruling Institutional Revolutionary Party (PRI). Caught up in the evolution from simple assembly plants to more high-tech plants, Mexican workers have also adapted to Japanese work techniques. Besides their greater flexibility, Mexican workers are cheap, often earning an average of only US$5 or US$6 a day.

After the 1982 devaluation, American dollars bought more pesos, making the *maquiladora* worker among the least expensive in the world. Furthermore, the 1987 wage and price control pact negotiated between the government, unions, and the private sector severely depressed wages in Mexico's fight to reduce inflation. It is this combination of low wages, flexibility and skill, American company owners hope, that will allow them to regain an edge over their evermore able competitors in the Far East, and to hold their own with the European Union. For such companies, the most important aspect of the North American Free Trade Agreement (NAFTA), which came into force in 1994, is that it 'locks in' Mexico's pro-business reforms, seemingly for ever.

General Electric, based in Fairfield, Connecticut, opened its first plant in Ciudad Juárez in 1971. Their electrical appliance division in Louisville, Kentucky, was finding that making the electrical cables which go inside their appliances was becoming too costly. Because of the time needed to make them, they were expensive and also, explains a GE spokesman in Mexico, 'the workers didn't like the job. If they could get moved to another department in the plant they would always take the opportunity.' With the success of the Juárez plant, GE decided to expand in Mexico, and now has eight plants there, employing 8,500 people. Various GE divisions now operate in cities such as Nogales, Juárez, Chihuahua City, Ciudad Acuña and Reynosa, where workers make circuit breakers, motors, coils and pumps, allowing GE to compete not only with other American companies that have *maquiladoras* in Mexico, but with the so-called Pacific Rim countries of Japan, Taiwan and South Korea.

Ironically, the Reynosa plant is the only GE plant that is unionised. But even GE admits that those who run the union, which is pro-government and pro-employer, have shown themselves to be far more intent on attempting to earn extra money through 'purchasing arrangements and other contracting matters', than representing their dues-paying members.

Nor is it hard to figure out why the Mexican government is so happy to see such explosive growth in the twin-plant industry. Originally they were set up to provide jobs and economic opportunities in the traditionally poor and underdeveloped border area. The border had long attracted immigrants or temporary workers looking for jobs in the US. When there was no work available, many came back to wait on the Mexican side of the border, usually in severe states of destitution. A workforce was therefore ready and waiting for the promotors of the industry. Yet it was rarely unemployed men who were hired to work in the new plants, but local women - new to industrial work, apparently docile, and cheap - who worked on the assembly lines.

Until the opening up of the Mexican Stock Market to foreign investors and its subsequent boom, the US dollars injected into the economy for local purchases and salaries were an extremely important source of foreign exchange for Mexico. With wages, administration fees and services, the *maquiladora* industry pumped US$4.8 billion into the Mexican economy in 1992, making it the nation's second-largest source of dollar earnings after foreign sales from the petroleum sector.

The *maquila* industry was also supposed to transfer modern technology from the First World to Mexico. It was claimed that the new methods and technology introduced via the *maquiladoras* would eventually spread throughout Mexican industry, but this has not happened. On average only two per cent of inputs in the *maquila* industry are provided by Mexican firms. *Maquila* operations can vary from a crude table with a group of people sitting around it to assembly lines fed by multimillion dollar state-of-the-art equipment, but in neither case does technology transfer occur. Foreign companies guard their technological advances jealously and, until the enacting of NAFTA, were they to sell the *maquila* machinery to a Mexican company, they would have to pay duty on it.

Some *maquila* watchers predict that NAFTA will destroy the *maquila* programme, citing the government's need for the asset tax and for more integration of foreign industry with Mexican industry. *Maquiladoras* will no longer be obliged to ship their products back out of the country, and with the Mexican market to sell to, they say, joint ventures and plants closer to the nation's populous central areas, such as Mexico City, make more sense. Already since 1988 *maquiladoras* have been allowed to sell up to 50 per cent of their output inside Mexico, although so far, very few of them have done so. Others have pointed out that the *maquila* programme benefits from being already NAFTA-compatible. While NAFTA removes all the old duty exemption programmes by 2001, items meeting the Agreement's rule of origin requirements will continue to flow duty free across all three borders.

For Mexico, the *maquiladora* programme, the 1986 signing of the General Agreement on Tariffs and Trade (GATT), the liberal foreign investment laws of 1987 and 1989, and now free trade with Canada and the US, all show its desperate desire for economic growth. For more than sixty years Mexico has relied on state-led economic development, known as import substitution. This has meant encouraging both Mexican and foreign manufacturers to produce in Mexico goods destined for the Mexican market, rather than relying on imports. In Mexico's case it has also entailed dependency on oil exports. Along the way, Mexico's economy has been left behind by other Newly Industrialised Countries, such as South Korea and Taiwan. Between 1980 and 1988, for example, the nation's Gross National Product (GNP) grew at only 0.7 per cent a year, less than population growth. Meanwhile an estimated one million people enter the workforce every year.

When the eyes of first world capital, particularly that of Europe, turned towards Eastern Europe and the former Soviet Union after the collapse of Stalinism in 1989 and 1990, Mexican president, Carlos Salinas de Gortari, realised that no-one outside the Americas remained interested in investing in Latin America anymore. Throughout the 1980s, in fact, only about 25 per cent of all the first world investment directed towards the Third World had gone to Latin America, according to Mexico City international trade expert Ruperto Patiño. In February 1990 Salinas was hard pressed to find an audience for his speech at the annual World Economic Forum in Davos, Switzerland. That was when he reportedly decided to take up US president, George Bush's, offer of talks on a North American Free Trade Agreement. As one Mexican economist puts it, 'The Mexican ruling class, after years of protected growth, feels confident enough - and that it's necessary - to compete on the world market.'

In fact, Mexico had already been transforming its economic strategy and opening its doors to foreign trade. In 1986, during the administration of Miguel de la Madrid, Mexico signed GATT, opening the floodgates to American consumer products, as well as machinery and technology. By 1992, Mexico's bilateral trade with its northern neighbour had grown to US$49 billion compared to US$21 billion in 1987, but the country's overall trade surplus had turned into a bloated deficit of US$21 billion. Over half of this was accounted for by Mexico's trade deficit with the US. Estimates for 1993 show the deficit remaining at US$21 billion. In February 1994, the president of the Mexican Association of Importers and Exporters, Juan Autrique, was predicting a massive overall trade deficit of over US$26 billion for that year, thanks to NAFTA and the tide of cheap US imports.

Salinas privatised the banks and 252 state-owned companies such as the telephone company, Telmex, the AHMSA and SIDERMEX steel companies, as well as railcar manufacturers, shipyards, and sugar refineries. He also tried to streamline the one state company the government says it will never sell, Petróleos de México S.A., or PEMEX, firing more than 100,000 workers in less than four years. The number of state employees fired since 1988 has risen to more than half a million. Over the last decade such measures, accompanied by massive cuts to social services and education, have turned a federal budget deficit of 16 per cent of GDP into a surplus of US$2.67 billion in 1993.

During the 1980s the Mexican government had to devalue the peso three times because of the debt crisis and other factors. By 1993, however, the peso was considered over-valued, by as much as a third according to some economists, making exports uncompetitive, imports cheap and stoking the trade deficit. Nonetheless, the overvalued peso, along with cuts in public spending and depressed wages, allowed Salinas to bring inflation down from a high of 179 per cent in 1988 to single digit levels of 8.1 per cent in 1993.

Inflation may have fallen, but the social cost has been huge. According to the UN's Economic Commission for Latin American and the Caribbean (ECLAC), the minimum wage is now worth about half of its 1980 value. A study by the Los Angeles-based Latin American Citizens' League shows that 40 per cent of Mexicans are malnourished, receiving less than the minimum recommended 2,750 calories per day. A 1993 survey in Mexico City by the National Autonomous University of Mexico found that 60 per cent of workers live in poverty.

The PRI has ruled without serious challenge since 1929 not only because of its skill in choosing whether to buy off the opposition or to use violence to quell it outright. It has also constituted itself - again skilfully - as the embodiment of the Mexican Revolution. It is, in more than just name, the revolution institutionalised, manipulating industrial workers, peasants, poor *colonia* dwellers, merchants and the business sector all for the good of Mexico, or rather, for the good of the Mexican elite. Along the way it has managed, in spite of its economic problems, to make Mexico one of the most stable regimes in Latin America.

But the PRI has been making it clear that it no longer intends to buy the lower classes off, even by the inadequate standards of the past. On the one hand, it still has the country's massive, corrupt union structure to keep unhappy workers under control. On the other, it is hoping that its recipe for a stronger economy - competitive, newly modernised companies making cheaper goods and hiring more workers, lashings of foreign investment, and severely curtailed public spending - will finally start to bring results and bring the lower and middle classes some of the buying power they lost in the 1980s.

By the end of 1993, with companies that had long depended on government patronage about to sink or swim in NAFTA's treacherous waters, it was apparent that much of Mexican business was in trouble. As the stock market boomed, small- and medium-sized companies found themselves choked by high interest rates, a slowing economy and competition from imports they couldn't match. A *Wall Street Journal* editorial suggested in 1992 that as much as two-thirds of the foreign investment coming to Mexico was 'short term investment in peso stocks and bonds,' speculative money that was not going to improve productive capacity. According to the National Council of Manufacturing Industry (CANACINTRA), 60 per cent of the nation's industry was in recession by mid-1993. In all kinds of plants, from ceramics to autoparts, as much as 50 per cent of capacity was idle. The informal economy, much of it little more than peddling goods on the street, took up the slack and now employs millions, accounting for at least 25 per cent of GDP, according to various studies.

Even though his free market reforms did not work out as well as he had hoped - the nation's GDP grew by a dismal 0.4 per cent in 1993 - Salinas pressed ahead with NAFTA. He not only needed free trade with Canada and US to reassure investors and open up markets, but most importantly, to cement his economic reforms firmly into place.

Along the way, Salinas has continually raised expectations, promising ordinary Mexicans that free trade would bring them prosperity, as it catapulted Mexico from the Third World into the First. Yet, if the *maquiladora* programme - and the society it has helped create along the border - is anything to go by, it seems increasingly unlikely that those expectations will be met.

❋ ❋ ❋ ❋ ❋

That August dawn in 1991, Petra left the factory alone. She managed to struggle past the Invamex hospital equipment factory and the three large Zenith plants at the entrance to the industrial park, before pain forced her to stop. Fortunately, Candi had also got permission to leave by then and found her.

Meanwhile word about Petra's tragedy had spread around the factory workers, reaching the union representative, Francisco Perera. Perera, a friend of Petra's, went to the chief of production, angrily complaining about the events. 'She's lost a litre and half of blood,' he told the production chief, adding that it was all the fault of supervisor Martín Ríos. The production chief agreed to send a company van and driver to take Petra to hospital.

By then the day shift was arriving at the plant. News of the dispute passed between the shifts. Backed by the workforce, the union rep went back to the chief of production and demanded that the supervisor be fired. That day, every shift went on a ten minute work stoppage in protest.

All 450 workers joined in, demanding that the company dismiss Martín Ríos. Instead the company called in the union reps from all three shifts, and told them they were fired. As far as they were concerned, said the chief of production, Petra hadn't had a miscarriage at all. She had merely fallen ill, and it had nothing to do with the company.

Back at the hospital, Petra was treated and told to take two weeks off work. She had been at home just three days, resting in her flimsy yellow house with the hanging plants and the pig and the upholstered board leaning against the roof, when the chief of personnel showed up in Colonia Roma, and told her that the plant manager wanted to speak to her. 'He took me in to the factory at ten, and I spoke to the three main managers,' remembers Petra. 'They told me that if I said anything to anyone about what had happened, I would be the one who ended up getting hurt, that I could even end up in jail.'

Petra took her fortnight off and returned to work only to find herself a pariah in the eyes of factory management. She had already been the kind of worker they didn't like; she worked hard but sometimes gave the supervisors a lot of lip. Like the time Martín Ríos came by with a broom and told her to clean up. 'He just handed me this broom and said, "Sweep",' says Petra.

'Well I didn't, because that's no way to ask anyone to do anything and that's not my job. So I told him to go sweep himself. He got mad and took me to personnel saying they had to suspend me without pay for three days. But they didn't and that made him think I was getting a laugh at his expense.'

Even today, Petra doesn't quite know why she didn't insist harder on being allowed to go, although leaving without permission would have cost her the job. Maybe it was the thought of those two mouths to feed that made her resign herself that night to doing what she was told. As Mary puts it, 'You're just obliged to swallow whatever they do to you.'

After returning to GE, Petra says, the first thing she saw on entering the plant was Ríos jeering at her. In order to get her to quit, the supervisors kept on her back, to work faster, keep up production, not to go to the bathroom, shouting at her and threatening to fire her, until finally after less than a month, she couldn't take it any more and left. Because she quit and wasn't fired, she got no severance pay from GE.

That wasn't too great a problem. There are lots of *maquila* factories in Reynosa, and Petra soon had a job at another, Lintel, a *maquiladora* which assembles telephones for an American company called Sinopac International. Within three months, however, Petra was pregnant again, and once company management noticed it, she says, they fired her.

Now Petra has three children and works in a shop, earning mostly commissions which add up to just over US$33 a week. She'd give just about anything to get an illegal job north of the border, maybe cleaning someone's house. Her *compañero* Oscar recently spotted her name on a black list - Petra has never been able to get another job in a *maquila* since being fired from Lintel.

Petra still remembers Supervisor Ríos with his round smug face and his smile when she came back to work after the miscarriage. She still remembers him coming over with the broom and commanding 'Sweep!' as if she were a servant. Which is why the long upholstered board is leaning against her roof. The sisters put it down on two packing crates to form a bench when they invite other *maquiladora* workers over to their place to talk about their jobs and what they can do to make sure the foreign plants respect their rights. 'I got involved with this labour rights group about two months after the miscarriage,' says Petra, 'because the whole thing made me so angry. Instead of punishing the supervisor, they punished me, as if I had done something wrong.'

Sitting under the meagre shade of the acacia tree, Mary talks about the latest events at GE. 'This year the union didn't even negotiate a contract for the workers,' she says. 'They haven't done anything. The situation here is much worse than in Matamoros. There the workers have united and here, they're afraid.'

Two young men, who also work at GE and have just put down US$100 for a plot of land and thrown together yet another plywood shack in Colonia Roma, talk about the nine-hour shifts, low wages and the heavy production schedule. A young woman named Ester who works at the W.R. Grace Corp *maquila* describes the bad air and how the women workers there frequently faint from the fumes. They spend all day inserting plastic tubes into intravenous bags at incredible speed, 36 per minute, she says, and if they drop more than three onto the floor, they get a report in personnel which could lose them a day's pay or cost them their jobs. 'So what everyone does is just pick them up off the floor again,' she says matter-of-factly, 'and send them on down the line.'

❄   ❄   ❄   ❄   ❄

The meeting lasts about an hour and a half. As they finish, the group makes plans to get together again the following week and invite others to join them. Says Mary, 'People know that they have to unite. That way they'll be stronger, they'll find the courage to confront the companies. That's why we've got to keep meeting and find a way to change our situation. Otherwise those American companies will keep stamping all over us.' By then it's time to go home and get ready for the afternoon shift.

[1] The list of 500 largest companies published annually by *Fortune* magazine.

2
Don Jaime's Domain
The Rise of the *Maquiladoras*

Don Jaime Bermúdez' office is tranquil and air-conditioned, a suite of rooms making an effort to be tasteful with prints of horses on dark green mats and large pastel arrangements of artificial flowers. Two impeccably dressed bilingual secretaries field phone calls and book appointments from large desks in the carpeted foyer. The view from the upper floor windows takes in the crowns of trees and the verdant lawns of the Ciudad Juárez Golf and Country Club.

As founder and owner of Grupo Bermúdez, 'a market-driven, full-service industrial organisation committed to attracting foreign development to Mexico,' according to its publicity brochure, Don Jaime is both the architect and the embodiment of the *maquiladora* industry in Mexico's first and still foremost *maquila* city, Ciudad Juárez. Businesslike yet affable, with a round innocuous face and slightly protruding front teeth, Don Jaime, 69, claims the credit as the founding father of the *maquiladora* programme. It began in 1960, he recalls, when his uncle, Antonio Bermúdez, was appointed head of the federal government's National Border Program, known as PRONAF.

Antonio J. Bermúdez had always had good connections with the PRI, serving as mayor of Juárez between 1941 and 1943, and becoming a senator in 1946. From 1946 to 1958, as director of the state oil company, PEMEX, and over two more years, after being appointed Plenipotentiary Ambassador for Petroleum, Antonio Bermúdez made extensive contacts with foreign businessmen all over the world. 'A group of us, we were fairly young at the time,' Don Jaime reminisces, 'went to see my uncle because we wanted to see if we could change the *modus vivendi* of Juárez. You know after the war, with all those US soldiers stationed in El Paso, the main business here was nothing but a kind of third-class tourism - cabarets, bars, houses of prostitution, gambling - and we wanted to see how we could change it.'

Bermúdez and his colleagues decided to commission a feasibility study from the University of Boston's business faculty, outlining a proposal to attract foreign industry to Juárez. Although a handful of *maquila*-type operations had been set up in border cities such as Tijuana and Nogales by then, for Don Jaime, 'that's really where the *maquila* industry was born. The [government's] Secretaría de Comercio in Mexico City liked and supported the proposal, but the fact is, aside from them, most people were dead against it and said it would never work.'

Mexican economic policy at the time, he remarks, was based primarily on promoting and protecting domestic industry - and on mistrust of American enterprise in general. Having done business in a border town for more than a generation - the Bermúdez family had long been involved in real estate and construction, as well as owning the Waterfil distillery and some nightclubs - Don Jaime had quite a different concept of his fellow entrepreneurs from across the Río Grande. 'We did business with them, traded with them', he says. 'The border was always different from the rest of Mexico in that regard. We didn't have that fear of selling out.'

Nonetheless, the process of lobbying for a free trade zone along the border took about five years. 'Finally, in May 1965,' explains Bermúdez, 'we got a letter from the Finance Secretariat allowing machinery and goods to be imported duty-free, establishing the right of foreigners to come over to manage the factories, and so on. We then spent the next two or three years promoting the idea to American companies. A few small factories came first. Then came RCA in 1968, and that was the breakthrough, the first big company, a household name.'

For Bermúdez and his colleagues - indeed for almost any entrepreneur living in a border city - the idea made sense. For many years the north of Mexico had remained an economic backwater, sparsely populated and, aside from mining and smelting, largely unindustrialised. There was little commerce, unemployment was high and for many Mexicans border towns were simply way stations *en route* to jobs in the US. Tourism, the main source of earnings in cities like Juárez and Tijuana, often included a whiff of the illicit or immoral. In 1915, in the middle of the Mexican Revolution, the *Boston Herald* ran a series of articles on Ciudad Juárez, emphatically (if ungrammatically) titled 'The Most Wickedest City in the World.'

Describing it as 'a second-rate Monte Carlo', the article accused the city of harbouring 'a swarm of swindlers, forgers, and crooks of low estate. Besides a rare collection of dope fiends and drunkards, Juárez is populated by vagabond soldiery...', it thundered. While the lowlife aspect of Juárez appeared typically Mexican to American eyes, in fact it was primarily American businessmen, suffering from the suppression of such activities in the US, who financed and controlled the city's bars and gambling dens. This was true of other Mexican border cities from Nuevo Laredo to Tijuana.

Fifty years later, very little of substance had changed in Juárez. Concentrated overwhelmingly in cities like Monterrey, Guadalajara and the capital, Mexico's post-war boom had largely eluded the border. Land values were low, unemployment was massive, and aside from basics like the airport and the railway, built in 1884, there was little infrastructure.

The *maquiladora* programme, says Bermúdez, was simply 'the logical thing to do. It made sense. American companies saved money. Mexicans got jobs. Everybody won.'

At the time, the American government was concerned about increasing numbers of Mexicans migrating to the US, who were willing to accept lower wages than American workers. Washington hoped that the US$4-a-day jobs south of the US border would keep Mexicans away from the upwards of US$4-an-hour jobs to the north. At the same time, this kind of off-shore manufacturing increased profitability for all kinds of US companies.

For the developers of the industrial parks the prizes were equally handsome. Urban land could be bought for a song, paved and developed with municipal funds, then rented out to foreign companies at a sizeable profit. The Mexican personnel and production managers would need new housing, paved streets and basic services. Business in the shops downtown and throughout the city would grow with the influx of workers and wide modern highways would have to be built to transport goods back and forth from the *maquiladoras*. According to sociologist Leslie Sklair, the operators of industrial parks and shelter programmmes - which take companies under their wing and provide them with plants and workers - can earn at least 50 cents per hour per worker, (roughly half the workers' own salary at current levels). For a 200-worker factory, that comes to about half a million dollars a year.

And so Don Jaime's idea caught on. In 1960, Juárez had a population of just over a quarter of a million; today it has an estimated million and half. In 1970, 3,165 people were employed in 22 Juárez *maquilas*; by 1974, 89 plants employed over 17,000.

Already by 1975 Mexico as a whole had captured 37 per cent of US investment in off-shore assembly of goods, ahead of traditional cheap labour nations such as Taiwan, which then held 29 per cent of the market, and Hong Kong, which held 13 per cent. As a percentage of total US-Mexico trade, the *maquila* industry accounted for 24.8 per cent in 1983, rising to 43.6 per cent by 1992.

The year 1982 was a turning point for the industry. That year the debt crisis hit Mexico, the peso was devalued, and employment in the *maquilas* jumped from 127,048 in 1982 to almost 200,000 two years later. The number of plants in Mexico rose from 605 employing almost 131,000 workers in 1981 to 2,129 plants employing 511,000 people by 1992. While the average number of workers per plant in 1974 was 166, according to SECOFI, by 1991, it was 242, and by 1993, 250.

According to the INEGI, the three most important sectors in the *maquila* industry in 1980 were electronics, textiles and electrical machinery, with 157 plants manufacturing electronics, 117 in textiles and 66 assembling electrical machinery. By 1989, electronics was still the largest sector, but autoparts had displaced textiles as the second largest employer. Between 1980 and 1986, for example, the transportation sector grew by 649.7 per cent, while textiles grew by only 7.7 per cent. By October 1993, electronics still formed the greater part of industrial activity, with over 20 per cent of the total. Textiles had recovered to a close second, with 411 plants out of the total 2,187, compared to 425 electronics plants.

In terms of employment, 345 electronics plants employed over 104,000 workers, almost a quarter of the total, in 1989, while 93,656 were employed in autoparts and transport equipment manufacturing. The three main sectors employed over half the workforce that year of 447,190 workers.

In the industry's early days, women formed the vast majority of the workforce. In 1975, they constituted 78 per cent of the total, falling to 63 per cent in 1988, and to just over 59 per cent in 1993. The fall reflects the changing composition of *maquila* industries, away from sectors which traditionally prefer to employ women. In 1989, for example, women made up 79 per cent of textile workers and 72 per cent in electronics, but accounted for only 50 per cent in transport. INEGI's 1993 statistics show employment of men increasing by 10 per cent that year, and that of women by only 6.6 per cent.

The main advantage the *maquiladora* in Mexico offers foreign investors is still cheap labour, with even the high-tech electronics and autoparts sectors, for example, often concentrating their most labour-intensive processes, such as cable assembly, there. Although, as labour economist Harley Shaiken has stated, 'in industries such as electronics a "second wave" of *maquilas* is employing more sophisticated production processes,' the industry as a whole tends to mix high- and low-tech plants. 'Even advanced facilities combine high-tech and labour-intensive processes', he writes in a 1990 study, with some estimates indicating 'capitalisation per worker of US$10,000 in the electronics industry, compared to US$5,000 for the *maquilas* as a whole.' Consumer and industrial electronics, along with autoparts plants, are the most technologically sophisticated and have been the fastest-growing sectors over the past 13 years.

In Ciudad Juárez alone, there are now over 130,000 employees in some 340 factories spread through and sometimes beyond the eight industrial parks dotting the city. Three of those parks belong to Grupo Bermúdez and boast paved roads, drainage, electricity and telephone lines. Grupo Bermúdez builds the plants themselves with their often rather kitsch facades - pseudo-Greek, or hacienda style with tiles and ornate ironwork - that have come to characterise these new borderland factories.

It is extremely rare for a company to allow outsiders to tour their plants, but persistence pays off with a few visits. Most of the plants this writer was able to enter were simple functional structures, large, clean, well-lit, with cement floors, metal or cinderblock walls, and production areas in corners or along the assembly lines. One exception, a textile plant which was closing down in Juárez, was far more antiquated and cluttered. Its brick walls had been painted a light orange colour, the sewing machines were far from new, and piles of old fabric were scattered here and there on the dusty floor. Compared to labouring in fields or working in older factories, or indeed to the kind of housing most workers live in, the new factories must seem modern and spacious. But interviews with workers from a variety of plants reveal another reality, that of heavy production quotas, monotonous work routines, bad air quality and unfair treatment by management, in sharp contrast to the *maquiladoras'* spick-and-span physical appearance.

Ciudad Juárez and other border towns had experimented with free trade on previous occasions, and local merchants had prospered from it. Often free trade status was only won after heavy political pressure on the capital, part of the faraway north's historical inconformity with the rest of Mexico since colonial times. Free trade in the past had meant that American shoppers would come south to buy, finding a better range of cheaper, higher quality goods imported tax free from all over the globe.

Paso del Norte, as Juárez was named at the time, acquired its first free trade status in 1885, when the Mexican government agreed to extend the *Zona Libre* already established further east in cities like Matamoros and Reynosa, to the state of Chihuahua and the west. At the time, Paso del Norte was little more than a small town with nine streets crossing the main avenue, three general stores, a run-down hotel and a few hundred adobe houses. In just a few years the city became renowned for its elegant department stores offering luxury goods such as silk and cashmere from Europe and the Far East. Many belonged to enterprising foreigners and employed up to thirty skilled tailors at a time. Thanks to its railway heading south, Paso del Norte became the main trade centre not only for southern Texas, but for the state of Chihuahua as well as most of northern Mexico. One year after receiving its free zone status, the value of foreign exports coming into Paso del Norte for sale or further distribution south had leapt from an annual US$2.5 million to US$8.7 million. Local industries such as milling and distilleries also flourished.

Although today it is hard to imagine from the scrubby desert landscape surrounding the city, more than a century ago the area was an important agricultural region, especially for fruit orchards and vineyards. Verdant and productive, the central border area had been known for its wines ever since the first Spanish missions were established there in the 17th century.

The availability of cheaper goods in Mexico ruined business on the

American side of the border. One El Paso newspaper lambasted the free zone as 'a monster devil fish ... reaching out its slimy arms and constantly becoming more threatening and dangerous.' Editorials frequently described its very existence as an act of hostility against the US. Mexican towns grew up to three times the size of the American towns across the border.

Opposition to the *Zona Libre* also came from inside Mexico, as both domestic manufacturers and merchants forced to pay the usual tariffs found themselves losing money, unable to compete with the flood of imported goods entering Mexico so cheaply via the border cities. These were the years of President Porfirio Díaz, known as the *Porfiriato*, when Mexican policy-makers bent over backwards to please foreign business. British, French and American companies made fortunes out of ranching, oil, railroads and mining, while doing nothing to alleviate the barbaric living and working conditions among the Mexican poor.

In 1896 the Mexican government imposed a tax equal to 10 per cent of regular duties on all goods coming into the north, and a further 90 per cent if these goods were to be sent on into the interior. In 1905, just five years before the beginning of the Mexican Revolution, the *Zona Libre* was abolished altogether. By then, El Paso del Norte had been renamed Ciudad Juárez, after President Benito Juárez who had holed up there for a time in 1864, while Napoleon III's cousin, Emperor Maximilian, ran the country and tried to figure out why the Mexicans hated him.

The end of free trade status battered the city's economy. An agricultural depression brought on by severe shortages of water in the Río Grande - caused by American farmers in Colorado and New Mexico siphoning it off up-river - compounded the region's problems. Unable to survive, many rural Mexicans emigrated to the US. Agriculture in the area, unless larded with heavy investments in irrigation equipment, has never been the same since.

By the turn of the century, Ciudad Juárez had resorted to the business that kept it going until the *maquiladoras* arrived - tourism. Even today tourism remains important. Soldiers from the Fort Bliss army base in El Paso, vacationing students, families from small towns in Texas and New Mexico, retirees wintering in the area - all come over to Juárez to watch bullfights and dog races or shop for crafts and cheap liquor. Doctors and dentists are cheaper in Juárez, as are all kinds of pharmaceuticals, some of which are banned in the US. Along Avenida Benito Juárez, dentists offering dentures for as little as US$100 vie for attention with discotheques sporting names like Curly's, Spanky's, Fantasy and Crazytown. Just off Avenida Lerdo stands the city's big covered market, surrounded by small metal tables and chairs regularly cruised by multitudes of wandering vendors offering bootleg cassettes, jewellery and hammocks.

The *maquiladora* industry in the 1970s transformed the city much as the

Zona Libre did in the 1880s. But this time the word elegant is inapplicable. If there is one architectural detail that symbolises Juárez, or indeed any other *maquila* border town, it is that of the bare grey concrete wall with rusty fingers of metal sticking skyward. The city's old cathedral and town hall are now dwarfed by cheap department stores and badly designed office buildings that never quite look finished. New eight-lane avenues have been built through the city, choking it with traffic, noise, and fumes. A project to beautify the strip of land along the river remains an unfinished eyesore with miles of wandering white balustrades, parched grass and dry fountains. Old buses rattle through a neglected, claustrophobic downtown crowded with street vendors and liberally dotted with rubbish, where they disgorge hundreds of *maquiladora* workers. Wearing the aprons or work jackets that entitle them to free rides, they crowd the narrow sidewalks and board yet more buses, heading for barren suburbs lying further and further out from the original city.

Surrounded by mountains and nestled in the wide pass which gives the US city its name, Ciudad Juárez is also known for its bad air, which it shares with El Paso. The US city is home to two oil refineries and the old ASARCO copper smelter, all situated within the city limits. Both cities are also centres of the used car market, clogged with ancient vehicles imported from all over the US which fill the trapped air with lead and carbon monoxide. Recent reports in the newspaper, *El Norte de Juárez*, warned of a plague of giant rats running loose in the Cuauhtémoc Market. Despite its current population of a million and a half, by 1994 the city still did not have a single water treatment plant. While its source of potable water comes from underground aquifers, the pipes carrying potable water and sewage run side by side beneath the pot-holed streets and are frequently broken.

That is not to say that all of Juárez is a blight upon the desert landscape. Around the Golf and Country Club, mansions nestle in oleander and bougainvillaea. Out along the main highways, expensive restaurants cater to wealthy guests. Even the industrial parks are almost always professionally gardened, with rows of trees gracing the avenues and wide lawns around the plants. Lately, the city fathers even saw fit to erect a monument to the *maquila* worker, an unprepossessing statue easily missed as one crawls along yet another bleak, traffic-snarled highway.

Companies such as General Motors, Ford, General Electric, United Technologies, Toshiba, Phillips, AT&T and a host of others, manufacture, assemble and test thousands of products in plants throughout the city. At least five companies are devoted to coupon processing for American products. While 'last touch' assembly is still dominant, more and more companies are taking advantage of the cheap, skilled labour to move other, more demanding parts of the production process to Mexico.

One recent and often cited example of how the twin-plant industry has merged into large-scale 'vertical' manufacturing is Ford's US$500 million stamping and assembly plant in Hermosillo, the capital of Sonora state, about 1,000 kilometres southwest of Juárez. There skilled workers produce and assemble Mercury Tracers and Escorts for the US market, and have consistently won international awards for quality. With about 40 per cent of the inputs into this Ford plant made in Mexico, the Hermosillo plant is not a *maquiladora*, but an example of how Mexico's reputation for skilled, cheap labour goes well beyond simple assembly.

The explosive growth of *maquiladoras* in Juárez in the 1980s, especially after the arrival of the autoparts *maquiladoras*, provoked a labour shortage. Companies such as GE, which has five plants in the city, started to look elsewhere and the industry engendered by Bermúdez began to spread to other border cities which in turn went through rapid industrial and demographic growth for which they were poorly prepared.

Almost all the companies in Juárez suffer high rates of employee turnover, as well as absenteeism. Monthly turnover rates of one in seven are common. Workers have serious problems in finding places to live and feel little loyalty to the workplace. They move around from plant to plant for reasons as minor as subsidised lunches or the presence of a company soccer team, then move again because they get an extra few pesos or free transport to and from work. In Juárez staff turnover is currently estimated at about 15 per cent a month and in Tijuana, 12 per cent. Compared to the US, where the median turnover rate is just 7 per cent, the problem is a serious one, and costs companies in Juárez alone an estimated US$16 million a year. Some factory managers have been known to drive out to the *colonias* to try and entice skilled ex-employees back to work.

Such methods hardly address the real roots of worker dissatisfaction. Wages stay depressed, and any organised attempts by the workforce to improve them are almost always met with sackings. Instead, the companies offer social diversions such as beauty contests, cooking lessons or sports teams, try to improve the food in the cafeteria, and add attendance bonuses to the wages. Companies want to ensure that they set the terms for keeping experienced workers and react with great hostility to pressure from the workforce itself.

With NAFTA signed, Don Jaime maintains that Mexico's next big challenge in industry is not wages but preparing its workforce more stringently. 'My idea for Juárez,' he says, 'is to establish high technology industries here. For that we need the most technically prepared and well-educated people. I think we've got three to five years to get ready for this. If not, the opportunity could pass us by. We won't be able to take advantage of free trade with Canada and the US.'

As the city of Juárez and the *maquiladora* industry on which it now depends have grown, the Bermúdez family has become fabulously wealthy.

Today, the Antonio J. Bermúdez Industrial Park and Grupo Bermúdez, which comprises 36 companies, are worth over US$100 million, all of it managed directly by Don Jaime and his American-university-educated sons, Jaime Jr and Sergio. They have built seven other industrial parks throughout the state of Chihuahua, carry out contract manufacturing and own a construction company which has so far developed 10 million square feet of industrial space in Mexico.

It certainly didn't hurt when Don Jaime ran for mayor of Juárez in 1986 and won. His three year mandate was controversial, especially regarding a big PRONAF project which had been built in the 60s. This unwieldy complex of convention centre, museum, theatre and craft shops was supposed to attract tourists out of the shabby downtown with its continuing emphasis on drinking and dancing to something slightly more highbrow. Bermúdez, however, tried to sell the complex, except for the museum, to a private company. Concerned *Juárenses* occupied the theatre for three months in 1987 to prevent its sale, but the rest of the buildings and nearby land have been sold to a development company called Inmobiliaria Mall de México S.A. for a new project called Plaza de las Americas, which will eventually incorporate an ice rink, cinemas, and a large shopping centre.

Yet despite the new development, most of the PRONAF shops are isolated and lonely, devoid of business or closed down altogether. Inmobiliaria Mall de México is having trouble finding tenants. Baking in the hot sun of the Chihuahua desert, the complex now resembles the set from one of those futuristic films about the world after a nuclear war.

Grupo Bermúdez remains undeterred. Its most recent projects include a ten-storey luxury condominium near the Country Club and and an 8,000-square-foot 'American-style' office park. Not far from the moribund PRONAF they have built Pueblo Mexicano, an upmarket three-level shopping mall. Mostly meant to attract US tourists, it is a bizarre reproduction of the kind of Mexican village that has never existed outside of Disneyland. Complete with *mariachi* bands at weekends, sprinkling fountains, acres of colourful ceramic tiles and stores selling the same crafts sold at half the price in the downtown market, it is yet another monument to unrestrained and dubious taste. The look may even have become a city trademark. The designer who fashions the glossy, revealing, and ultimately tasteless gowns that grace the cover of *Cosmopolitan*, lives in, and is obviously inspired by, Ciudad Juárez.

While Bermúdez may believe that he created a situation 'where everybody won', the *maquiladora* programme has its losers in Juárez too. One of them is Elizabeth Macías, who lost her 16-year-old son, Julio, in a grisly industrial accident in 1990. It happened on the night shift after his first week at a plant called Autovidrio S.A., which manufactures windscreens for Ford cars.

Macías, 37, doesn't fit the part of a grieving mother. She has fluffed out bottle-blond hair, likes to wear tight jeans and a lot of makeup, and is rarely without a cigarette. For a while, after Julio's death, she ran a hair salon in Zaragoza, a Juárez suburb, a tiny place with a couple of ancient barber chairs and an open bible among the combs and hairdryers on the thickly painted white counter. Now, like many Juárez women, she has an illegal job in the States.

Macías has never lost her anger at her son's needless death and is determined to seek justice. One late afternoon, about eight months after Julio was killed, she heads off with Gustavo de la Rosa Hickerson, a Juárez labour lawyer, to talk to a man named Enrique Trejo. They find Trejo chatting with a friend in a scarred and junk-filled mechanic's yard on the Zaragoza highway, among a lot of other scrap yards adorned with signs which immediately explain the meaning of the Spanish slang, 'Yonke'.

In the past, lawyer de la Rosa has dealt with a number of cases where either serious injury or death was caused by company negligence. 'Industry in the modern world has been obliged to raise its safety standards because of the possibility of being hit in the pocket over health and safety,' he says. 'That doesn't exist here. The *maquilas* are extremely dangerous because they can kill people and it won't cost them a thing.'

Trejo had helped install the conveyor belt system at Autovidrio, and was there when Julio's crushed, lifeless body was found between two of the belts that carry away scrap. It was he who had to dismantle the machinery to extract the body. 'We told the company when we installed the line that they needed to put in safety screens as well,' Trejo tells Macías and de la Rosa. 'But for two years they said not to bother. After the boy was killed, they had us install the screens.'

Macías sits on the hood of de la Rosa's truck, listening to Trejo with a strange sad look on her face. It is as if she is thinking, 'I should never have let him go, I should have been a better mother'. The impression lasts only a moment. Macías wants to sue Ford, so does de la Rosa, and Trejo promises to sneak a camera into the factory and take some photos as evidence. He's quitting in a few days, anyway, he says, so he doesn't care if he gets caught.

Macías has always been dirt poor. Julio was the middle child of three; an older son lives with and supports Macías' mother, and the youngest, Verónica, goes to school bearing the family's hopes that someday one of them will get a good education and a decent future. Macías' ex-husband is an alcoholic and drug addict, she says, who has never given her the slightest help for their three children. She gave up on him a long time ago. 'He's crazy after all these years I'm sure,' she says, 'just a delinquent. Julio liked to go and visit him sometimes, but I haven't seen him in years.'

Macías supported her children by getting occasional jobs cutting hair, mostly going to the homes of a few faithful clients. The three of them lived in a one-room house in the Las Flores *colonia* in Zaragoza, and by the time he was 16, says Macías, Julio had had enough. 'He got desperate,' she says, 'he said to me, "Living like this makes me sick. I want to get you a proper house and help you do something".' Since Julio was too shy to go by himself, they went together to Autovidrio to apply for a job for him. Julio's age was no problem; four out of ten workers in Juárez *maquiladoras* are under 20.

On Friday 31 October, Julio went in for the night shift, looking forward to his first paycheque. He was planning to take some of it to buy a pair of shoes the following Saturday. At some point he was sent to sweep up in a part of the factory that was idle during the night, even though he had been hired as a line operator, not a janitor. Trejo thinks he might have been trying to clear some kind of obstruction where the rollers of the two conveyor belts met and got stuck, then crushed, jamming the machine. No-one really knows because Julio was alone.

Julio's fellow workers passed around the hat and got about US$200 for the Macías family; his paycheque went to help pay funeral expenses. The company offered about US$300 compensation, and from the Mexican Institute of Social Security, she began to receive a monthly pension of US$20. The idea that her son's life was worth so little finally drove Macías to sue the American head office for damages, something no-one had done before in Juárez.

The case went to court in El Paso in 1992, presented by a lawyer named Robin Collins. According to Collins, Ford argued that, although Autovidrio was indeed a subsidiary, the head office was not responsible or liable for what went on there. If they wanted to sue someone, they should sue Autovidrio S.A.. 'But together with that notion of the corporate shield [that legally protects the head office],' says Collins, 'there is also the legal concept of piercing the shell.' Therefore, he countered, the law allows them to go to court and prove that the corporate shield idea is a just a legal dodge, that in fact, Ford built, directs, and controls the plant.

Collins says that, aside from winning Elizabeth Macías compensation, he hoped to use the case to accomplish two wider goals. One was to expand upon a Texas Supreme Court ruling of 1990, which says that foreign-born nationals working for American companies have the right to sue for extra-territorial injuries. The other, he says, was 'to establish for a whole group of fleeing American corporations that if they were going to continue to do this, they ought to be held accountable to US notions of occupational safety.'

While Macías waited for news, driving back and forth across the border in an ancient Nissan so wrecked its keys fall out of the ignition every time she hits a bump, Ford filed for delays. Collins was worried about the case. The first person to find Julio's dead body was, according to Collins, the kind of worker 'who wakes up in the morning and thanks God for Ford'. This witness said that Julio was wearing a 'Niggers With Attitude' cap that night, and that NWA had been written on the ceiling over the belt, suggesting that Julio had climbed up to such a dangerous position in order to scrawl the graffitti.

❋ ❋ ❋ ❋ ❋

People like the Macías' don't get rich working in the twin plants; they don't even become middle class. Trekking out to the newer settlements that have sprung up around the city presents the observer with sweeping vistas of shacks - some wood, some cardboard, some brick, most a motley combination - in disordered rows among the rocks and hills and weeds. In December 1993 alone, seven children living in such places died from the cold.

These are the homes of the people who remember the city's other history, not as a haven for reformers like Benito Juárez or free zone entrepreneurs, but as the centre of operations for Pancho Villa during the Mexican Revolution of 1910 to 1920. With its railroad, customs house monies and proximity to arms dealers in the US, Juárez was strategic for Villa and his *División del Norte*, the Northern Division that swept down to Mexico City to defend the gains of peasants and workers in the first years of the Revolution. While *Villistas* fought federal troops in the streets of Juárez, the curious citizens of El Paso would line the river bank to watch, many falling victim to stray bullets in the process.

Pancho Villa, and Emiliano Zapata in the south, wanted to see real changes for the mass of oppressed and impoverished Mexicans after the revolution, not merely the overthrow of a corrupt president. But as the fighting continued their demands were diluted and eventually codified in a series of weak laws designed to give peasants small and often barren bits of land, known as *ejidos*, and industrial workers a few reforms designed to set limits on their exploitation.

One of those reforms was the creation of INFONAVIT, a government department for workers' housing. INFONAVIT homes today cover small parts of Juárez in neat, pastel painted rows of block-and-plaster houses complete with doors and windows and running water. In theory, employees can contribute a portion of their wages to INFONAVIT, then take part in a raffle to win a house. In reality, the vast majority of those lucky enough to acquire an INFONAVIT house are the better off; government employees, small business owners, and families with at least one member working in the US.

Many of the poor *colonias*, which have names like Emiliano Zapata, Oasis of the Revolution, or Mexico 68 - in reference not to the Olympic games of that year but the massacre of students in Tlatelolco Square which preceded them - are controlled by rival political parties. In spite of their poverty, inhabitants must pay a *cuota*, or monthly due, to the community leader. Usually, people are told that this money is to pay for services such as water, electricity, or paving, but years pass and none of these amenities appear. More often than not, the money goes instead into the pockets of the community leader or their political allies.

Residents are expected to support and vote for the party that controls the *colonia*. One party, calling itself the Peoples' Defence Committee (CDP) and professing leftist leanings, has made a business out of keeping anyone supporting the right-wing National Action Party (PAN) - the main electoral rival of the governing PRI - out of the poor districts. In return, government customs officials turn a blind eye to their massive imports of used clothing, and hundreds of vendors licenses have been distributed to CDP members.

The Labour Party, or PT, also controls some *colonias*, along with the PRI. During the 1992 elections for the mayors and governor of the state of Chihuahua, the PRI not only allowed but actively encouraged thousands of *maquiladora* workers and recent arrivals to invade vacant lands on the outskirts of the city. But the areas to which they were sent were the worst possible for human habitation, right up in the mountain folds that surround the pass. Even had the PRI won, there was no way that the municipality would have had the money or political will to put in any kind of basic service in such geographically impossible areas. In the end, the PRI lost the elections for both the state of Chihuahua and the city of Juárez to the PAN, and now hundreds of families are stuck in inhospitable suburbs of quickly erected shacks, travelling hours to and from work. One woman from one of the new, unplanned settlements complains, 'We went crazy trying to put up this house. On what you see now, just in cardboard and wood, we spent about US$350. We owe money to every single relative we have, and the municipality told us they would take care of everything.'

It was in one of the ramshackle colonies in the suburb of Zaragoza controlled by the CDP that a woman named María del Carmen Rodríguez lost her four children in 1989. Carmen's husband had left her a few months earlier, so she applied for and got a job with a twin plant called Maquilados Técnicos, making aluminium tubes. With wages that didn't allow her to put her children in daycare, and the government-run nurseries already full, she kept her oldest, an eight-year-old boy, home from school to look after the three younger ones including an eight-month-old baby. Like hundreds of women workers along the border, to make sure they didn't escape and get into trouble, she would always lock the door of her cardboard-and-wood shack before going to work. One cold February morning, just after she had left for the factory, her shack exploded. Newspapers reported that Carmen Rodríguez had rigged up a small electric heater with telephone wire. The heater burst into flames, which sparked off another heater, this one working on butane gas, and blew the place apart, instantly killing all four children. Carmen's neighbour, Lourdes Morán, said she looked out of her window that morning because she thought it unusual for the sun to rise so early. 'But the glow through the curtains was not the sun,' she recalls. 'It was the house on fire.'

It is one of the ironies of the *maquiladora* industry that while it was ostensibly established to deal with unemployment, the majority of those who found work there were young women, entirely new to industry. While the percentage of male workers has risen over the years, the double burden of work and raising families placed on women *maquila* workers is probably the chief source of social problems in border cities. Even when children do not meet the tragic end of the Rodríguez family, the human cost of poor care and a life of grinding poverty is still high. Many leave school at 15 or 16 and go to work in factories themselves. Others roam around with friends, sniffing glue or taking drugs. Some start selling drugs, which are ubiquitous on the border, at the gateway to the largest drugs market in the world.

Hugo Almada, a sociologist at the University of Juárez who carried out a 1991 study of conditions in the so-called *colonias populares*, calculates that there are 50,000 gang members in the city. An astonishing 60 per cent of youngsters between eight and 24 in these districts use some form of drugs, including glue. 'It's so bad,' he remarks, 'that when you go to the *colonias*, you can pick out the kids who are *not* sniffing glue. It's that dramatic.'

About a third of working women, who in 1993 still formed 59 per cent of the *maquila* labour force, are single mothers, according to Almada's Juárez study. 'They have nowhere to leave their children,' he explains, 'so most either leave them with a relative or friend or locked up in the house all day. The number of children going to Juárez highschools has actually dropped, in spite of the population boom, because they are either working in *maquilas* themselves or are totally uninterested in school.'

❋ ❋ ❋ ❋ ❋

A study by researchers at the Northern Border College in Nogales, Sonora, found that the average family in the *colonias* has two or even three salaries coming in. To make ends meet, many workers also get into some kind of merchandising, whether snacks on the street, candy or popsicles on the city bus routes, or second-hand clothing and other goods in the neighbourhood. One textile worker in Juárez recounts that his factory once nearly went out on strike because the management moved the work day ahead by a half hour. So many people there had second jobs that the change would have wrecked the careful daily juggling act of their constant search for a few more pesos.

One logical result of such a hopeless situation for many *Juárenses* is the continued attraction of jobs across the river. Illegal immigration is higher than ever and blatant, despite the helicopters and hundreds of border patrol officers. Behind Juárez,' ugly city hall, brash young ferrymen called *pasamojados*, literally 'wetback runners', run a thriving business floating Mexicans without documents across the cemented-in, knee deep Río Grande on inflated tyre inner tubes, at about US$1.50 a trip. The telltale sight of damp shoes or trouser legs in downtown El Paso is the quickest way back to Mexico, courtesy of the Border Patrol.

While from the *colonias* of Juárez the gleaming office and hotels towers of downtown El Paso may look like some southwest version of Manhattan, the American city is itself is one of the poorest in the US, with an estimated one quarter of its population living on food stamps. Per capita income is about US$9,000 and over ten per cent of the population is unemployed.

Nonetheless, the Border Patrol has its hands full searching for Mexican maids working illegally to earn their US$50 a week, highschool students, street vendors, part-time construction workers, and Mexicans without temporary permits who cross the river to join those with permits to spend all day picking grapes or chilis in the blazing sun for less than the US$4.25 an hour minimum wage.

In summer and autumn the streets of El Paso near the international bridges downtown are filled with men and women sleeping on the sidewalks on pieces of cardboard, waiting for the early arrival of buses that will take them west to the farms in New Mexico's Mesilla Valley, or east to Fabens. In 1992, a strike broke out when New Mexico farmers cut the price paid per bucket of chilis from US$1.25 to just 85 cents. The Border Patrol was used to break up pickets. One outraged resident complained in the local paper, 'That poor La Mesa farmer that all those people are striking [against]. Don't those people realise that farmers don't have that much money? Send them back to Mexico.' Yet as the industry grew from US$54 million in 1990 to almost US$60 million in 1991, the price paid to New Mexico chili farmers by the packers actually went up in 1992.

❊ ❊ ❊ ❊ ❊

As far as Don Jaime Bermúdez is concerned, however, wages in the Juárez twin plants are not low. 'They're higher than in China, for example,' he points out. He adds a comment common in business and government circles in Mexico. 'People have to understand that they can't just get higher wages without higher productivity,' he says. Yet studies show that workers' productivity has not been met by improved wages. According to University of California at San Diego economist Harley Shaiken, while 'productivity rose by 41 per cent between 1980 and 1992, the wages and benefits of a Mexican manufacturing worker [in 1992] were only 68 per cent of what they were in 1980, a low level to start with.'

'These have been difficult years for the economy and you can't change things overnight,' persists Don Jaime, 'If the salaries of factory workers go up, what about the doctor's or lawyer's secretary? It would cause great imbalance in the economy. It may hurt for a while, but it's necessary.'

For Elizabeth Macías, free trade, *maquiladoras* and the rest are just one more way to take advantage of Mexicans. 'I couldn't care less about this free trade thing,' she comments several months after Julio's death. 'It won't help anyone but the rich.' With free trade negotiations still going on, she says that Americans should come down there first and see the harm the companies were causing the Mexican people. 'Mexicans work because they have to earn a living,' she exclaims, 'not to be killed. We're human beings and we have the right to live. Our children have the right not to have their lives cut short.'

In March, 1993, Ford made an offer of compensation to Elizabeth Macías, not because they were admitting responsibility for her son's death, but to stop the suit against them. Part of the settlement terms required that the actual amount be kept confidential. As far as Ford is concerned, Julio 'was grossly negligent and, in all likelihood, the sole cause of his own death.'

The Texas Supreme Court ruling giving foreign-born nationals the right to sue for extra-territorial injuries was effectively neutralised by the Texas state legislature the same year who passed a law saying that 'it was not convenient' for them to do so. And the idea of making US companies responsible for injuries and health hazards in their Mexican plants was quashed by the Free Trade Agreement, which stated that the previous system would prevail.

Elizabeth Macías' final words on the matter are damning. Factory workers and their families have to organise and start fighting back, she says. 'That's the only thing they can do, because for sure the government will never do anything for us.'

3

Women's Work

Attempts to Organise

Ever since the *maquiladora* factories began springing up in the north of Mexico, wages and working conditions have been a source of conflict between workers and foreign companies needing to keep costs down. Throughout the years of industrial growth, *maquila* workers have never given up trying to extract better wages and more control over their working lives through organising, strike action and other means. But they have continually run up against the brick wall of management intransigence, the corrupt union structure, and frequently, government connivance with both.

Much of this movement for more rights and better conditions has been built and strengthened by women. When the *maquilas* first started up, they employed vast numbers of women workers, and today they still make up well over half of the *maquila* workforce. The history of their struggles is often a story of defeat, but it is also a picture of resistance that illustrates the potential for change.

❄ ❄ ❄ ❄ ❄

Matamoros, a city of 500,000 in the northern state of Tamaulipas, still has a small town feel to it, settled in the last meandering bends of the Río Grande before it empties out through a wide and sandy delta into the Gulf of Mexico. The bridge connecting the city to Brownsville, Texas, bustles with cars, trucks and people, with customs posts and offices at either end trying to control the traffic. In the afternoons, streams of Mexicans hurrying back with heavy packages of groceries and other goods from US stores pass American tourists carrying striped blankets, onyx wind chimes and ceramic statues of bulls and Bart Simpson, heading the other way.

Downtown Matamoros is a jumble of old and new; small wooden cottages adjoin walled-in, two-storey brick structures, cheap taco stands alternate with giant shoe shops, noisy old saloons with swinging doors and lazy overhead ceiling fans vie for custom with modern marble-fronted hotels.

Dozens of *herbaria* shops offer medicinal remedies and good luck charms to crowds of shoppers. Every day a boy on a bicycle selling the newspaper, *El Fronterizo*, rides through the streets announcing unusual events and scandals through a tinny-voiced loudspeaker. There is an old theatre, the *Reforma*, complete with arches and a big, wood-panelled foyer, and, a few blocks from each other, two squares lined with trees. The Old Square and the New Square, people call them, although the Plaza Vieja hasn't looked old since a hurricane in the 1980s tore out all its mature trees.

María Guadalupe Torres has lived and worked in Matamoros almost half her life. She is a short, slightly portly woman with curly red hair tied up in a pony tail, and pale freckled skin. At 49, she has never married and still lives at home with her mother, Doña Petra. For almost 20 years, Lupe, as all her friends call her, was an assiduous worker in one of the two Kemet capacitor plants founded by Union Carbide in Matamoros. When she retired six years ago, the plant manager came to her home and asked her if she would like a more responsible job in plant security. But Lupe had to turn him down. She didn't tell him why exactly, but the truth was, she already had a new job. She was running the Border Committee of Working Women in Matamoros, and would be active from morning to night setting up meetings and organising other *maquiladora* workers. The people Lupe talks to are the kind of people Kemet would like their security personnel to keep out of their plants. They complain about labour law infringements, want everything that is owed them, and already form the nucleus of a movement for the kind of independent trade union that will one day do these things without Lupe's informal classes.

If Don Jaime Bermúdez personifies the *maquiladora* industry, Lupe, and many others like her, encapsulate the twin plant workers' determination to organise and press for change. Among many stories of struggle, that of the women workers of Matamoros proves that the nascent working class along the border has never been and will never be content with US$5 a day. But it also shows the equal determination of both the company head offices and the Mexican government to stop them at all costs.

Lupe Torres was born in Cárdenas in the state of San Luis Potosí. Perhaps her self-reliance can be traced back to the way she and her mother have always had to fend for themselves. Lupe's father, a railroad worker, was killed in a train accident when she was only months old. Doña Petra survived by doing domestic work for other railroad families in return for food and lodging, and so Lupe grew up sleeping on floors in the corners of other people's shacks. She dropped out of primary school and went out to work at the age of ten. When she was 16, Lupe and her mother got domestic jobs over the border in Brownsville, Texas, but after about ten years, both moved back to Mexico where Lupe started working in a pottery factory in Matamoros.

Her first factory job was a painful introduction. After her first week, she was informed that the first two weeks of employment were considered training and therefore unpaid. Lupe demanded her wages, got them after a lot of argument, then promptly quit. Her second job was in a workshop making knitted handbags, where the women sat on sheets of newspaper on the floor to work. In 1969 she got the job at Kemet, but the move from small Mexican-run shops to the large multinational company brought no improvements in her working conditions. At Kemet, Lupe worked in the injection moulding section, making capacitor bodies from epoxy and washing them in methylene chloride, a highly toxic chemical. Lupe remembers that the chemicals carried warning signs in English, which no-one could read.

Lupe had been working for Kemet for 12 years when one day in 1981 she saw a poster on a wall announcing a talk in a church hall on the Federal Labour Law. At the time, she recalls, 'life in the factory was unbearable, because of the shouts, the aggression of the supervisors, including one American. We were always watched, we weren't allowed to talk to each other at work. I had to work with strong chemicals without gloves. I had begun to ask myself, what can I do?' Lupe talked to 15 *compañeras* from the factory and persuaded them to attend the meeting with her even though, as she explains years later, 'I really didn't know what it was all about.' The information, all of it from a thick government tome, was a revelation. 'It was the first time,' she says, 'that I realised that as a worker I had rights. Until then, with my upbringing, I had believed that all I could do was serve, produce and obey, without the right to reply. Those meetings gave me courage and self-esteem. I would go, taking in more and more ideas, first with people from my factory, then I'd meet women from other factories, from every *colonia* in Matamoros. A lot of them were afraid at first. But when I realised what benefits we could achieve, I realised that was what I wanted to do. We were opening people's eyes, forming new groups everywhere.'

In Matamoros the percentage of women in the workforce is particularly high. It used to be close to 100 per cent, and even now, Lupe estimates, is about 80 per cent. Unlike in other *maquiladora* cities, every one of its factories is unionised, a legacy from the city's days as a cotton-milling and shipping port. The *maquila* workers union is called the SJOI, the Spanish acronym for the Union of Dayworkers and Industrial Workers. Everyone from musicians to waiters is attached to a union, all of them under the umbrella of the government-controlled CTM, or Mexican Workers Confederation. When someone needs to apply for a job, they go to the union office, where they are told which workplaces are looking for employees.

❋   ❋   ❋   ❋   ❋

The CTM was first formed in 1936, during the presidency of Lázaro Cárdenas. From its early days, under the leadership of its first general secretary, Vicente Lombardo Toledano, the politics of the federation were closely tied to those of the Mexican president.

Lombardo had previously worked closely with the infamous Luis Morones, leader of the rival CROM, or Regional Mexican Workers Confederation. During the post-revolutionary regimes of presidents Alvaro Obregón and Plutarco Elías Calles, who took power by defeating revolutionary heroes Emiliano Zapata and Francisco Villa, Morones had crushed independent unions and forced them to join his federation. Morones grew fabulously wealthy for his troubles and was at one point rewarded with the post of Minister of Labour.

When the CTM was founded, its methods compared favourably with the violence of the CROM, and it won the initial support of many workers. Yet it soon stamped out any vestige of democracy within the organisation. President Cárdenas was bringing in reforms that the poor of Mexico needed, but was under siege from his party's right wing, which preferred the more nakedly aggressive measures of the past against workers and peasants.

Lombardo worked to organise the Mexican working class and bring it to Cárdenas' side. He used the rhetoric of revolution, railing against US imperialism. He visited Russia, supported Stalin, and declared himself, 'a Marxist, but not a communist.' But his politics had little to do with the liberation or empowerment of the working class.

All movements for strikes or wage improvements had to be approved first by the CTM leadership. To encourage foreign investors, as well as help Mexico's state-owned companies, such as the recently nationalised oil company, PEMEX, such actions were usually blocked. In 1940 Lombardo wrote, 'the federal government has intervened in every important strike'. Within a few years, the CTM and Lombardo had managed to stamp out almost any independent organisation among the Mexican working class.

In 1943, one of Lombardo's most conservative henchmen, Fidel Velásquez, became leader of the CTM. Now in his 90s, eccentric and at times incoherent, Velásquez continues in the post, exercising total control over the CTM and demanding unblinking loyalty to the ruling PRI. Today the government, through its Labour Arbitration Boards originally founded in the 1920s, continues to intervene in all strikes, grievances, and workers' movements.

Ever since its inception, CTM regional and local leaders have been appointed by a tightly-knit group at the top with direct connections to the government. For years the CTM-appointed leader in Matamoros was a powerful political figure in the local ruling PRI named Agapito González Cavazos. Now 77, González began his career as a typical table-thumping

CTM *cacique*, or all-powerful local boss. But starting in 1978, a series of events occurred which rocked his secure place in local politics.

On 25 June 1978, riots broke out in Matamoros during a protest over the jailing of a student by a new chief of police, a friend and nominee of González. The police chief's reputation for brutality included one accusation of murder. Students began the protest and thousands of others soon joined in. The crowd set fire to the local jail, the headquarters of the PRI, and the town hall, and were about to head for the CTM hall when the riot was finally quelled, leaving four students dead. 'It was a great blow for Agapito', recalls Lupe.

At the same time one local PRI leader, Matamoros mayor Enrique Cárdenas, decided that the union held too much sway in the party, and tried to reduce González' influence with a series of attacks against him in the press. A year later, the city's voters ousted Cárdenas, voting overwhelmingly for a popular candidate from a rival party called the PARM, the Authentic Party of the Mexican Revolution. But by then, the damage was done. 'Agapito knew that, having lost so much influence, if he were to lose the SJOI, he'd have lost everything,' says Lupe. 'And meanwhile, the women were organising.'

According to Lupe, the women had begun working discreetly inside the factories, meeting after hours to discuss which of their needs was the most urgent. 'We didn't want to go to the union with a long list of demands because we knew they would just say no,' she explains. At that time there was a good deal of criticism of the union and the CTM. 'In one hundred per cent of our meetings there were always criticisms of the union, very serious ones,' she recalls, 'but we realised that we had to separate the criticism from the strategy.' A group of women would then go to the union hall and describe a problem, rather than demand specific actions. They would be firm and resolute, says Lupe, but refuse to get into an argument.

In June 1983 a breakthrough occurred when Marina Reyes, a member of Lupe's group, went with a handful of women to the SJOI hall and told Don Agapito that they couldn't live on the miserable salaries they were being paid and would very much like to have a pay rise of 50 per cent. González scoffed that their demands were pretty big compared to their small numbers, and that he couldn't help. The following day, Marina returned with 900 women. They filled the assembly hall of the three-storey union headquarters, with its big Mexican flag portraying González, Fidel Velásquez, and the President in its tricolour sections. González had no choice but to meet them. He agreed to tell the companies to increase wages, but that 50 per cent would be impossible, so he would try for 25 per cent instead. With one voice, Lupe remembers, every woman shouted 'No!' Within days, González had informed the companies that they would have to increase wages by 50 per cent or the factories would go out on strike. The women got their raise and established a hold over the union structure that grew as time went on.

The constant push from below on both the union and the companies by the largely female workforce has made the *maquila* workers of Matamoros the highest paid on the border. Wages are about double those paid anywhere else, with pay for weekends included in the 40-hour week, the shortest working week in the *maquila* belt. Every year wages are automatically adjusted for inflation. All factories have two-year contracts which are always renegotiated with a raise. Holidays are paid with a bonus and many factories get extra paid holidays. The city has two large well-run nurseries, free for the children of women workers. Men and women workers alike are largely aware of their rights, and make sure they get vacation pay, maternity leave, and so on. Calculating that the 35,000 workers employed in Matamoros *maquilas* earn on average an extra US$20 or US$30 a week over other cities, people have between US$35 and US$50 million a year to spend, boosting the local economy.

Yet by not directly challenging the corrupt structure of the union, or its ties to the government - something which Lupe believes the *maquila* workers were not yet ready for - the women still needed González' backing to keep up their progress. It proved a fatal weakness.

Early in 1992, Don Agapito was negotiating new contracts with *maquila* management. Contract talks were going poorly and workers were preparing for a strike. A few had already gone out on strike, quickly winning their increase because the factories had orders to fill and they were operating on the 'just-in-time' system where money is saved by keeping low inventories and filling contracts as needed. Late one night, police arrived at the union headquarters, charged González with tax evasion, and arrested him. He was put on a plane to Mexico City, where he remained for eight months. After some complicated legal manoeuvring by his lawyer son, also named Agapito González, the union leader was released and returned to Matamoros, but since then his willingness to fight the companies has been noticeably depleted.

Cirila Quintero, a young researcher with the Northern Border College in Matamoros, believes that US management didn't mind the union set-up in the city. They had an excellent workforce, practically no employee turnover, and the wages were still ridiculously low compared to those at home. 'And when the economy really was bad, Don Agapito would be flexible and lower the demands,' she points out. 'The people who really didn't like González and wanted to get rid of him were the local managers, the Mexican businessmen in the Maquiladora Association, who felt the union was deterring foreign companies from investing.'

Since González was spirited away the union has begun to mirror more faithfully the stance of the CTM-controlled unions in the rest of Mexico, putting the needs and wishes of the companies before those of its members.

The January 1992 demand of a 20 per cent raise was watered down to 8 per cent. According to Lupe Torres, companies are now trying to extend the 40-hour working week without extra pay. The women of the Border Committee of Working Women used to give classes in labour rights in the union hall itself; now they have had to head back out to the *colonias* to speak to small groups of men and women workers.

Early one Saturday morning, Lupe takes a crowded bus to the home of Dora Elena and Betty, two young women sharing a tiny rented brick house with Dora's brother in one of the hot, muddy *colonias* that sprawl over the semi-tropical land around the city. All three work in factories in the city's industrial parks. Dora Elena, 21, has asked Lupe to come, she says, 'because of all the injustices I see going on at my plant every day.'

Betty, 25, is from Matamoros. She worked as a maid for a while in Houston, Texas, and now makes plastic forks for McDonalds restaurants in a factory called Textex. Dora and her younger brother are from Tampico. After her three-month maternity leave, Dora has just returned to work at KHL Industries, the automotive wiring plant where she has been employed for the past five years. She sits on one of the large room's double beds with her newborn son, Erik. The other half of the room is taken up by a rack of clothes, a lumpy couch and armchair and a television set. Through a curtained doorway lies the kitchen, and beyond that, a small yard.

A friend of Dora's brother, a young man named Armando who works in a metal stamping plant, also joins the meeting. Wielding her plastic covered copy of the *Ley Federal de Trabajo* like a bible, Lupe begins the meeting with a series of questions about what companies can and cannot do. The lesson quickly develops into a general discussion about all aspects of their jobs, vacation time that isn't paid, a man who has been laid off six days without pay because he stayed home with his sick wife for two days, and what to do about a friend of Betty's who has been fired for no apparent reason after four years at Trico, a Buffalo, New York-based company that manufactures the electronic components for windscreen wipers.

They also discuss what is going on with the union. According to Betty, the girl from Trico went to the SJOI to complain, but was told just to sign the resignation form and worry about it later. 'That's the last thing she should do,' retorts Lupe. 'Once she signs that form, she'll have lost any right to ask for her job back or get decent severance pay.'

'That's what I thought,' replies Betty, 'and when we were at the union office, I went to the library to ask the woman there if she had a copy of the Federal Labour Law, and she didn't know what book I meant. So I said to her, "you know, that thick paperback book with a purple cover." But she still couldn't find it.'

Afterward, Lupe walks across the street to the house of a young woman named Inés, who was also at the meeting. Inés, now working for the

Committee, was previously employed at Zenith, where her mother, Magda, still works. When it arrived in Matamoros in 1969, Zenith was the first big plant to set up operations in the city, and is still one of its single largest employers. Picking her way over the packed dirt road, Inés describes the kind of problems women workers have been having at the plant. Fifty have been laid off temporarily without pay and another 50 lay-offs are on the cards, yet the company is advertising for new staff, preferably female, between the ages of 16 and 30. Older women who have been working for the company for over ten years are being sent from the department assembling television tuners to *pistolas*, where they have to glue together extremely tiny components. Since this work requires excellent eyesight and very quick movements, many of the older women can't get used to it, says Inés, and are being fired for not keeping up production standards. Worst of all, the company has begun to punish workers who are working too slowly or else complaining about the situation. They are being told to spend the entire day sitting on a bench against the wall outside the nurse's office, and do nothing. Some women have spent weeks not working, just sitting all day on the bench. Not surprisingly, most of them couldn't take it and have quit, losing their severance pay.

Inés is also worried about whether her new job might get her into trouble. Lupe tries to reassure her, 'Look, everything we talk about is just the law of the country. There is nothing illegal about it. What happens is that companies come here and don't even want to obey the law that gives us our rights. They are the ones in the wrong, not us.'

❄ ❄ ❄ ❄ ❄

Chicago-based Zenith has *maquiladora* plants all over the north of Mexico, including several in the next big city west of Matamoros, Reynosa, where their Plant #13 is the city's largest. Workers here also attempted to win better conditions and a more democratic union in a 1983 strike that affected the whole city.

Reynosa seems more fast-paced than Matamoros, dominated by the metal towers and smoke stacks of a huge PEMEX refinery. Its built-up downtown area is bland and functional, its roads busy with traffic heading to the giant industrial city of Monterrey and other points south.

In an outlying suburb known as Colonia Almaguer, the Ramírez family have a one-storey house on a corner lot, shady with fine-leafed huisache trees. Angela Ramírez, 29, worked at Zenith years ago, and for her the strike is a part of her life that she'd rather forget. Neatly dressed with long dark hair, she seems calm and very serious. She usually prefers not to talk about the event, but one morning, in the family living room adorned with large wedding pictures of married brothers and sisters, she goes back over those events of 1983 as if recounting a story from a newspaper.

Here too, the Border Committee of Working Women had begun to hold meetings on the Federal Labour Law in a vacant church hall. A Zenith worker named Daniel López, who worked the morning shift at the plant and drove a small bus at nights, had found out about them and grew interested, taking fellow workers to the meetings in his bus on his free nights. The CTM union leader here was a man called Ernesto Jauregui, and when he found out that people were going to the meetings, and that Daniel López was taking them, he feared he had a rival on his hands.

In early November 1983, an article appeared in the local Reynosa newspaper saying that López was a criminal who had kidnapped a lower-ranking union leader. The following morning, police arrived at the factory to arrest López and take him to prison, an act witnessed by hundreds of workers. At the end of the day shift a large group of Zenith employees, mostly women, went to the jail, hoping that their presence would keep López safe from maltreatment or torture by the police. The group outside the jail grew when the afternoon shift arrived from work. Together on the street, they started talking about going on strike. According to Angela, it was only a small group who originally wanted to go ahead with the idea. 'There were only about a dozen or fifteen of us,' she recalls, 'but because of what was happening, more and more people decided that we should go out, until we had a majority.'

The Zenith workers knew so little about their country's labour laws that they didn't wait to channel their demands through the Arbitration Board. They decided to go out on strike straight away.

Their demands were simple. They wanted Ernesto Jauregui sacked and clean elections for a new leader, the release of Daniel López on the trumped-up charges, and a wage increase. By then, it was 4.30 on the morning of 7 November, and they wanted the strike to start with that day's morning shift. They quickly had to find red-and-black flags to put up on the factory gates, the traditional sign that the workers are on strike and the plant closed, so a couple of women took off their slips, which happened to be red and black, tore them up and sewed flags.

'The people of Reynosa supported us in the strike,' says Angela, 'and that was really important. They came to the picket lines with coffee and sandwiches. They donated money so people could buy groceries for their families. The whole city was with us.' By the following day, every *maquila* in Reynosa had come out in sympathy. The CTM had a crisis on its hands and Fidel Velásquez himself came up from Mexico City to see what was going on. Finally the CTM agreed to call free elections and Daniel López was released from jail. The wage increase was refused. The elections took place the following Sunday, and the reformers won 82 per cent of the vote.

But unknown to the reformers, a lawyer representing the union had signed a note saying that Velásquez had final say over the vote results. The note was legal and Velásquez simply annulled the vote. Shortly afterwards, many workers, including the strike leaders like Angela, were fired. Others were threatened and harassed, and the movement fell apart. Daniel López now works as a bus driver full-time, and Angela, disillusioned by the whole process, never worked in a *maquiladora* again. Her case for unjust dismissal has been pending with the Labour Board in the state capital, Ciudad Victoria, ever since. 'A lawyer from Ciudad Victoria told me he would take care of it,' she explains, 'but I've really never paid much attention. I got a job as a hairdresser for a few years, and now I work as a secretary for a school.' She no longer cares what goes on at Zenith.

While the strike and its aftermath have left a bitter taste for Angela, her niece Aurelia, 19, is not content to let things lie. Aurelia, a tall, thin, fast-talking young woman with curly red-tinted hair, has been working at Zenith for a year, and according to her, conditions are probably worse there now than in Angela's day. 'I only get US$33 a week,' she complains. 'We were promised a 20 per cent increase last January, only it's never come. In fact, they took 5,000 pesos off our weekly pay. In February, we started to get angry about it, and stopped work for a day, on two assembly lines.' A number of people were then fired and a group of them went to the union to complain. 'But they just said we'd better not make trouble,' she adds, 'because people were taking our photos and we'd be fired. And they said, "you'd better not come out on the First of May parade with any signs about it either".' According to Aurelia, both the union and the supervisors say that Zenith is having financial problems and that if the workforce don't accept the status quo, the company will just close down and move elsewhere.

Since the 1983 blow-up at Zenith, the CTM has kept a close rein on the *maquila* workers in Reynosa, and has even pressed companies to sack union members who they identify as trouble-makers.

Aurelia goes to meetings on labour rights and constantly broaches the subject with people at work. 'There are lots of things that go on there that are unfair,' she says. The most common question from union members is where their union dues end up, a question which the union has never answered. 'I stand up for myself pretty well, and for others too. Some people get really upset the way the supervisors shout at them, saying things you would never expect an educated person like an engineer to say to a woman.' Living with her aunts and grandparents ever since she and four brothers and sisters were left orphans in a car crash 15 years ago, Aurelia says she wants to save what money she can to go to university to become a lawyer. 'I'd like to do labour law,' she said, 'and do something to help workers, not like those lawyers who work for the union.'

❄ ❄ ❄ ❄ ❄

Angela Ramírez' sentiments are widely shared. In 1992 a survey in Mexicali, Baja California, of workers who had taken part in local strikes, asked whether they would consider going out on strike again. The entire sample replied 'no'. 'Some were promised a victory and keeping their jobs, only to find that they lost the strike, lost their jobs, and that it took them a great deal of time and effort to find new work,' says Leticia Figueroa, the sociologist who carried out the study. 'Others have no confidence in the union leaders and feel totally disillusioned.'

The demoralisation and distrust of unions uncovered by the Mexicali study is repeated among *maquiladora* workers in cities all along the border. In Ciudad Juárez, lawyer Gustavo de la Rosa laments the fate of one union whose members have organised and forced through clean elections five times, only to have the new union leaders bought off each time. In Juárez, the country's oldest *maquila* city, there are now only a handful of pro-government unions left and practically no-one campaigning for alternative, democratic ones. Instead, workers in *maquilas* have come up with a novel way of pressing for higher wages. A group of workers in one plant forms a coalition, hires a lawyer, and informs the local Labour Arbitration Board that they wish to go out on strike if the company will not negotiate. Once the issue is settled, the coalition then dissolves.

Like de la Rosa, for whom she worked for 11 years, Graciela Erives is a Juárez lawyer who handles numerous such coalitions, shepherding the petitions through to the Labour Board and giving advice. Graciela, 42, originally from the small town of Junta de Chihuahua, used to be a *maquila* worker herself. For nine years she sewed clothing in a factory called Acapulco Fashions before being fired after a spontaneous strike erupted in 1978.

'The factory had a union, but it was undemocratic,' says Graciela, who has been practicing law for 13 years now although she has never gone to university. 'They charged us dues, but never once had a meeting and the leader was appointed in Mexico City. But I had always liked to read about law, especially labour law, and I always defended my rights in the factory. One day, the supervisors came over and told us we had to work overtime the next day, even though it was a statutory holiday. I knew that it was illegal, and I said so to the manager. What's more, we hadn't been paid that week and they said we wouldn't be getting anything until the following week. A group of us had a meeting and talked about it, and then I found out that another group was doing the same thing, so we got together and decided to close the factory doors. I hadn't been leading anything as such, and all kinds of people were speaking their minds, but the company needed to blame someone so they said that I was the instigator and fired me. I brought my own case to the Labour Board, and won it, then started a study group with other women about the labour laws.'

A few years later, recounts Graciela, the owner of Acapulco Fashions died and his family took over the plant. They mismanaged the business, and soon the banks were at the factory doors. 'I realised what was coming so I entered a petition with the Labour Board, on behalf of the workers, to go out on strike,' she explains. 'This meant that the property was automatically closed. No bank could come in and confiscate machinery in lieu of the company's debts. Instead, the machinery was sold to pay the workers' vacation and severance pay.'

From then on, Graciela began to work as a lawyer, eventually starting a practice with Susana Prieto in 1991. State law in Chihuahua allows two types of law to be practiced by unqualified people who 'have the confidence of the plaintiff,' according to Susana. 'One is penal law, and the other is labour law. That is how Graciela has been working all these years.'

It is the summer of 1992, and Graciela has been working on the case of 84 workers fired from a company called CCE, a *maquila* belonging to the Warren, Ohio-based Packard Electric division of General Motors. Packard has several plants in Juárez, and is known for paying much less than its competitors. 'Packard basic operators get US$4.50 a day,' says Susana, 'while in other electrical wiring and automotive parts plants here, workers doing the same job get up to US$8.80 a day.'

Detroit auto makers started setting up *maquiladoras* in the 1960s, but as the challenge from Japanese-made cars sharpened in the 1980s, moved ever more plants to Mexico. In 1987 General Motors opened 12 new plants in Mexico, while closing down 11 factories in the US and laying off 29,000 people there. During the 1980s, Ford restructured and made many of its parts suppliers independent. GM, however, has kept its suppliers in-house, one reason why it is, with 50,000 employees and nearly 50 plants, the largest *maquila* employer in Mexico. Its Packard Electric Division alone has 26 twin plants along the border.

'The CCE workers formed a coalition in May this year,' explains Graciela, 'requesting better working conditions, a wage rise, and benefits such as free meals, INFONAVIT housing, and the mandatory profit shares that are stipulated in the Federal Labour Law.'

Those interested in joining the coalition met secretly at first, according to Graciela, gathering the signatures of 10 per cent of the workforce needed to present a petition with their demands, while leaving the rest of the workers safe from scrutiny until the vote for the strike came up. At that point, they went to Graciela's law firm, and she prepared the petition to be sent to the Labour Board, informing them that if the company did not enter into negotiations, in six days the workers would strike. Before the six days were up, the 84 workers were fired.

According to the two women, no-one in the company should have known the identity of the 84 workers listed on the petition, only themselves and the members of the Board. 'Obviously, we would never inform the company of who was on the list,' says Graciela, 'so we can only assume it was someone from the Board.'

Graciela sued to get the jobs back of the 84 workers and won her case, the first time such a case has been won 'in 20 years of *maquiladoras* in Juárez,' Susana proudly says.

The next day, a small group of the fired CCE workers meets in Graciela's sparely furnished wood-panelled office across from a large shopping centre. They range from top-of-the-scale production technicians, who carry out the same duties as a supervisor and manage up to 50 workers for just under US$10 a day, to a 19-year-old line worker who assembles electrical harnesses for just over US$4. Yet their complaints are identical; low pay, unfair treatment and poor conditions.

For 25-year-old technician José Luis González, married with two small children, the wages he received over five years at CCE were a bad joke. His wife worked the morning shift while he went in for the afternoons, all to pay the US$100-a-month rent on their two-room apartment in downtown Juárez and other expenses. Between the two of them, their neighbours and relatives, they manage to have someone always looking after the children. 'It's just a way of living, or rather of surviving,' he says of his job. To make matters worse, when González was fired in May, his wife was harassed into quitting shortly afterwards.

Another coalition member, Ramón Cobos, 32, has worked at CCE for nine years, and earns US$15.70 a day, while his wife works as a nurse at another *maquila*. The family of four has managed to acquire an INFONAVIT house near the Juárez airport, but they had to borrow heavily to buy it rather than paying premiums and winning it through the usual lottery. 'In all the years I've been working at CCE, they've never had a raffle for INFONAVIT houses for the workers,' he says, 'only for company administrators, supervisors, or *personal de confianza*,' he adds, referring to the name commonly given to faithful, pro-company staff promoted into key positions in the factory.

Josefina Reyes, 27, joined the coalition from another of Packard Electric's Juárez plants, called Río Bravo II, where she is a production technician with 50 workers to manage. Since being fired after 10 years with the company, she says that she would be happy to accept the legal severance package and look for a job elsewhere. But the company has offered her only about US$75, instead of the US$1,300 owed her by law. 'It's not fair,' she complains. 'I was last earning US$7 a day, and it's a wage that you really have to earn. Because you have to come up with a whole lot of things that they're demanding - efficiency, quality, production. And afterwards, when you've given everything you've got, they send you away with next to nothing.'

The coalition members in Graciela's office have a catalogue of complaints. One is the terrible quality of the food served in the company canteens. 'Often it's a friend or relative of the managers who gets the concession to sell food,' says Josefina, 'and they're under no obligation whatsoever to make sure it is nutritious or varied or anything else. So you end up having to buy food from the stands outside, which costs you about US$2, almost half a day's wage for some people.'

When an assembly line worker injured his hand at work, Josefina sent him to the Mexican Institute of Social Security (IMSS) for care. When he returned with a paper to be signed by the chief of personnel, Josefina was called in for a dressing-down. 'You work for us, not them,' she was told. 'You should have said that the accident was caused by the worker's own negligence.' That way, she explains, the company has to pay lower insurance premiums to the government health system.

For the CCE workers, a union was not the solution to such deeply-rooted problems. With the bad reputation that unions have among workers all over Mexico but especially in the north, they have no faith in them as a way to improve their working conditions and wages. 'Here in Mexico, the unions are no good,' says Ramón Cobo. 'The only ones who get any benefits at all out of unions are their general secretaries. I think the coalitions are better, that and workers just knowing their rights.'

But Graciela reckons that no more than 5 per cent of *maquiladora* workers in Juárez know their labour rights, 'a tiny minority, and that's the companies' trump card.'

Not only the foreign companies but the Mexican government prefers the status quo. The last thing Mexican private or state companies want is to see wages rise in the *maquiladoras*, setting off demands among their own workers for parity.

Nonetheless, Graciela remains convinced that *maquiladora* workers' awareness of their exploitation is growing. 'The number of individual and coalition demands with the Labour Board goes up every year,' she points out. But the Boards are beginning to set a dangerous new precedent, in some cases denying the right of non-unionised workers to form coalitions. 'The question is, how far is their policy going to go?' she asks. 'Is it just a few individuals on the Board or something generalised? It could get to the point where people will get so fed up that they will start calling wildcat strikes instead of going through the legal process.'

'It's difficult to see what will happen next,' adds Susana. 'How many years did the Indians suffer under the Spaniards before rebelling and winning their independence? It's the same situation now.'

When asked what they can do about such a daunting array of problems, one CCE employee jokes, 'Take up arms and start a revolution'. 'Start another uprising like Pancho Villa,' adds another. Ramón Cobo is less radical. 'People need to be better educated about their rights,' he says.

In January 1993, 69 CCE workers were allowed to return to work. The rest had already accepted the company's offers of severance pay. The fight with Packard sparked off demands in other GM plants, but new coalitions got mixed results from the Labour Board hearings. 'When they saw that we had won,' says Graciela, 'that made them realise that they could win too.'

❄ ❄ ❄ ❄ ❄

Besides being one of Mexico's major and, given its aggressively squalid nightlife, most puzzling tourist attractions, the city of Tijuana in Baja California is also the site of the country's second-largest *maquiladora* industry. Here, the industrial parks and ramshackle workers' housing stretch as far as the horizon in all directions, climbing the barren grey mesas on which the city of about one million is built. In Tijuana *maquila* workers succeeded in organising and founding the industry's first and only independent union, at a plant called Solidev Mexicana, in 1979.

In one of the city's many cheap markets, María de los Angeles Altamirano, 32, owns a stall selling ladies' underwear. Back in 1979, when still in her teens, María played an instrumental, if accidental, role in the birth of the union. Thirteen years later, sitting cross-legged on a long wooden table surrounded by the beige, white and black undulations of C-cups and D-cups, she relates the story.

When not yet 16, María got a job working in a plant with one of her sisters, a *maquila* with about 300 employees belonging to Solitron Devices, making semiconductors for the Pentagon, US State Department, ITT, and Honeywell. When she started work, says María, she saw that the largely female workforce at Solidev was becoming increasingly unhappy. Aside from the desperately low wages they took home each week, the women were also suffering serious health problems from all the solvents and acetone with which they were working. At one point, recalls María, two of her fingernails became so infected that a doctor told her he might have to remove them. She asked to be transferred to a different department but it was impossible to escape the fumes and chemicals. 'We realised that women had been giving birth to babies who were sick, deformed, or mentally retarded,' she explains. 'Other workers suffered from bronchial problems, burns on their hands and so on. The supervisors never told us that the chemicals we were using were dangerous, and never ever gave us masks or gloves or anything, no security whatsoever.'

By 1979, an even more insidious practice had come to light. Many of the women at Solidev were being sexually harassed by the manager and other male staff. Usually, the manager said that he was a doctor and insisted on 'examining' all new female employees. When María's turn came, she had already been working at Solidev for a year. 'One day,' she remembers, 'a female supervisor came over and told me that the manager wanted to speak to me in his office. As I was leaving my workplace, a couple of the girls asked me where I was going, and I told them. I didn't know what what was going on at the time. I guess I was just pretty naive, but no-one had ever told me, probably because they were so ashamed. But the two girls and this guy named Jesús who managed the stockroom knew and they followed me to the offices. Inside, I was told by the secretary just to go on into the manager's office, and so I did. I sat there and asked him why he was locking the door. The thing is, I never suspected anything because this man had always been very nice to my sister and me, knew my parents, and even came with his wife to my sister's wedding. But suddenly he threw himself on me. I got hysterical, shouting and crying, trying to get the door open. But none of the secretaries outside would open it. Instead, my friends from the line arrived and heard me shouting, and they forced open the door. I ran out crying, still hysterical, and the whole factory saw what was going on.'

That same night the Solidev workers formed their union, something which, according to María, many women had already been talking about because of all the other grievances accumulated over the years. Two or three days later, they sent a petition asking to form an independent union to the Labour Board along with a warning that they were planning to strike.

'There were various issues,' says María. 'We wanted better wages and benefits because the salaries here in Mexico have always been like this,' - she holds up her thumb and index finger close together - 'that's why all these foreign companies come here, to operate without any protection for their workers, to avoid paying taxes, and to exploit Mexicans.'

From the outset, the workforce was determined to keep the union independent, wanting nothing to do with any of the corrupt union hierarchies that dominate Mexican labour. 'From the moment we saw how the authorities protect these people, and how they let the companies do whatever they want, we knew we didn't want to join any union mixed up with them. We knew they would only pressure us to give in to the company.'

At first, explains María, the company and the Labour Board said, 'OK, go on and strike. In two days you'll be back begging our pardon.' But the nascent union quickly gathered support from people all over Tijuana and even in the US. Striking workers collected donations at street corners and on buses, then ensured that the neediest got the money to pay their rents and buy groceries. Shops donated food and the students at the university also supported them. 'We had donations coming in from all sides, we could hardly keep track of them all,' says María. 'We got support from other *maquila* workers, from the people of Tijuana, and the whole state of Baja

California.' With this material and moral support, the Solidev workers stayed out until their demands were met, and won for themselves a 40-hour working week, with a pay rise, better conditions and more benefits.

The new union encouraged all its members to come to meetings, bringing their children if necessary. They went around to other factories to talk about the advantages of an independent union, uncorrupted by money and government influence. The idea proved popular and many *maquila* workers asked to join the new union. 'The authorities didn't like that,' says María, 'They realised that the American companies would finally have to start paying a decent wage, and that didn't suit them at all.'

The government and the *maquiladora* association realised that they had a major problem on their hands. A year of repressive tactics which included everything from harassment at the work place to threats against family members did no good. Sometimes, says María, while the members of the union central committee were waiting for a bus, a car tried to run them over. Police watched their houses round the clock. 'But we wouldn't give in,' she recalls. 'In the end the only way they could break us was by closing the factory down altogether. A group of us went to San Diego to try to talk to the Solitron Devices manager, but he told us to get out of his office or else he'd call the *migra* [US Border Patrol.]'

In early 1982, Solidev closed down one department and fired 50 workers. The factory went on strike, which the local Labour Board refused to recognise, while company management tried to divide the workers by offering some of them money or better jobs, and insisting that the union affiliate with a body called the Revolutionary Confederation of Workers and Campesinos (CROC), which in turn demanded that all its members had to join the PRI. Between September and October 1982, the company began removing machinery, and on 1 February 1983, closed the plant down entirely.

'For us at that time,' says María, 'it seemed impossible to leave a struggle that we had been carrying on for so long, but when they closed the factory there was nothing we could do. Like people say here, "With the dog dead, that kills the rabies."'

In spite of this disastrous blow to their growing movement, many of them wanted to keep going. But anyone having anything to do with the now-defunct union was threatened with being blackballed from the *maquila* plants as María and other central committee members had already been. The city's student organisations and leftist political parties were also watched and harassed. That's when María decided to open her market stall. 'You might be willing to sacrifice your family's needs, go to jail, keep meeting and keep fighting,' she says, 'but if you don't get some kind of response from people, who for economic necessity are just not able to take the risk and join you, then you can't do anything. It's like banging your head against a brick wall. That's why I say, if in Mexico we had better education and were more aware of our rights, we'd open our eyes. We wouldn't be afraid.'

María has not worked in a *maquiladora* since, but she still has her reputation. Every now and then, women from the city's factories come to her stall and talk about the Solidev union. They describe the problems at their own plants and ask for advice. That's why, says María, getting up to attend a customer, 'I'm convinced that the movement will start up again. With the right orientation and organising and support, I know we can win.'

4
The Way the Wind Blows
The Environment

Like the rest of her Colonia Uniones neighbours in the city of Matamoros, Teresa Méndez García can tell which way the wind is blowing by sniffing the foul air she breathes every day.

It is a hot still Sunday and Teresa is sitting in a small back room where she keeps her sewing machine and tailor's dummy. 'We can tell because we know what these factories are making,' Teresa explains. 'When it comes from the Preservation Products plant, it is a very strong chemical smell; it gives you a headache and you can't stand breathing it for very long.' That's when the wind is coming from the South-West. A slight change eastward brings the pungent odour of ammonia from the Stepan plant next door. 'The one that affects us most days,' she adds, 'comes from Retzloff, and then the breeze stinks of pesticides or insecticides.'

Families first started moving to this neighbourhood in the north of Matamoros about 30 or 40 years ago, escaping the seasonal flooding that made life a misery in other lower-lying parts of the city. In recen t years, with the arrival each month of more and more new migrants looking for jobs either in the *maquiladora* plants or in the US, Uniones spread even further.

Ten years ago, chemical factories like Brownsville-based Retzloff, Chicago-based Stepan, and Delaware-based Preservation Products began to replace the old sorghum and cotton warehouses along Avenida Uniones, a wide street that cuts through Matamoros and forms the southern boundary of the *colonia*. They produced wood preservatives, pesticides and chemical products such as concentrated chlorophenols and hydrochloric acid. Ever since the plants set up, in a long row behind chain link fences and thin stands of oleander, families have been putting up with the daily emissions, as well as several gas leaks and explosions. 'It has been affecting us little by little over the years,' says Teresa. 'People have begun complaining about asthma now, and stomach pains are common. You just feel kind of sick every day.'

Teresa, 38, works at her home on Avenida Central all day, sewing dresses and uniforms for private customers, office staff and bank tellers, working in the back room of the rambling one-storey house she shares with her parents and a brother. A tidy little woman with short, carefully coiffed hair and a slightly nasal voice, she comes across as quick-thinking and articulate, the kind of woman who makes the city's environmental officials groan when they see her striding towards them. Teresa never actually planned to become an activist, but foul air she breathes every day has made her into one.

After dark on Avenida Central and many other streets, people have to keep their windows closed, even on the most sweltering summer nights. Since people began complaining, the companies have switched to operating at nights hoping the protests would stop. 'There are times,' says Teresa, 'when I've gone out at one or two in the morning and you can see this dense white cloud in the dark sky.' Recently, she had to drive relatives to the airport late one night to catch a flight. 'When we went out to the car,' she said, 'they couldn't believe how bad the smell was. They said, 'How do you put up with this?' I just said, 'Well now you know what we've been fighting against here.'

The possibility that the air they breath could eventually cause cancer or some other disease is just one of the concerns of the people in Colonia Uniones and the surrounding neighbourhoods. Another has been the frequent accidents and leaks. 'People are waiting for the next one all the time,' says Teresa.

Since it set up in Matamoros, there have been six leaks from Retzloff, including a serious ammonia gas leak in October 1983, when sixty people had to be hospitalised. Back then, the streets in Colonia Uniones were not yet paved and so thick with mud that they were impassable to the ambulances. 'It happened at night,' says Teresa. 'The whole *colonia* had to be evacuated. People were running out on foot, children got lost, and quite a few people fainted. The bad smell stayed for two or three days after that.'

A few months later, when local reporters visited the site, they not only found a strong smell that made them sick, but took photographs of toxic wastes being dumped onto open ground on plant property. They also interviewed the director of the city health centre, Dr Gilberto Yarritú, who admitted that constantly breathing the fumes from the plant carried a serious risk of chemical poisoning.

In December 1990 another explosion, this one involving two tanks of chemical gas used to make insecticide, sent dense, reddish clouds over the panicking city, and some 90 people to hospital. Hundreds more complained of nausea and headaches. Without giving any reason, plant security guards and manager Arturo Ledezma refused both police and firemen permission to enter the plant for two hours.

There have also been leaks and explosions at Stepan and Preservation Products, according to Teresa. In one day alone, in June 1991, there were four leaks, from both Retzloff and Stepan. 'Nobody told us or tried to warn us,' she says, ' neither the police nor the company engineers nor the managers.'

One evening the following November there was a leak of monochlorophenol gas from Preservation Products. 'The smell went right into the centre of town,' says Teresa. 'We went to the plant and waited until midnight for someone from the SEDUE [the federal environment agency] to arrive, but the company wouldn't let anyone inside. At nine the next morning we went to the SEDUE office to complain, and after a few hours the SEDUE engineer arrived and told us it was all under control and we could all go home. Instead, we went back to the factory - he didn't even get there until one in the afternoon.' Teresa said that she'd heard that Preservation Products had been given a year to relocate, but that year has passed and nothing has happened. 'No-one obeys the laws here,' she says dryly.

Yesterday, Teresa and her neighbours noticed a particularly bad smell in the air. After some initial inquiries, they found out that it was coming from a large tank of chemicals that supplies all the city's industrial parks, and which is cleaned every six weeks or so with a deodoriser. 'People noticed the bad smell, and were beginning to vomit and get bad headaches,' she recalls. 'The phone was ringing off the hook with people wanting to know what they should do.' A group of them decided to go to the site both to complain and see what was being done. While there, a local radio reporter stopped them and began asking questions. Teresa overheard one environment official comment to the reporter, 'I don't know why you want to interview them. They're just a bunch of housewives who don't know anything.' Later, she adds, 'the municipal firechief told me that we were all exaggerating, because the deodoriser they were using wasn't even toxic. So I asked him, well, if it's not toxic, then why are all your men over there throwing up?'

Gas leaks have occurred in other *maquiladora* cities apart from Matamoros. In Mexicali for example, the Química Orgánica plant, a subsidiary of a Monterrey-based company, has released toxic acidic gas into the air four times since 1987. During the July 1990 leak, a plume of sulphuric and hydrochloric acid forced the evacuation of ten thousand people. The 45-mile-per-hour winds that day blew the toxic cloud towards the US side of the border, but officials there were not notified of the incident for several months.

Forty-three people were hospitalised, most of them small children, on the occasion of the latest release, in January 1992. Following that accident, Mexicali residents held demonstrations until SEDESOL, the new environmental department replacing SEDUE, finally shut down the plant permanently, one of the few times such an action has been taken. Química Orgánica, however, announced that it would simply relocate.

In Juárez in March 1991, a truck carrying sulphuric acid sprang a leak while travelling through the town centre, spraying and injuring various bystanders on the street.

Just outside the city of Reynosa, a *maquila* called Metromechanica makes batteries in a large grassy area dotted with weeds and small trees near a *colonia* named after Francisco Villa. Out here the homes are small but well built, with much more space than most such districts provide. Yet Metromechanica dominates the *colonia*. People say they suffer regularly from pains in their ears, throat, and stomach. They too have to keep the windows of their small homes closed at night, preferring to put up with the heat and suffocation than the strong smell of acid permeating the searing summer night air outside.

One young man in Francisco Villa who worked at Metromechanica for a while gets out a couple of his old pay stubs. He says he couldn't stand the smell of acid any longer and quit. The plant paid no more than a bare minimum wage, he adds, and since the constant acid burns turned his unprotected clothing to rags, it was costing him too much money to work there. About a week earlier, a fire at the plant had further alarmed the people of Francisco Villa. Black marks and smoke stains from the fire can still be seen on the rather rundown-looking plant's metal walls. In the past, residents of the *colonia* have complained to the environment department many times, increasing their calls and visits after the fire, but so far nothing had been done.

❊   ❊   ❊   ❊   ❊

Across the river in Brownsville, just a few miles away from Colonia Uniones, Guadalupe Esparza, 21, lives with her husband Steve and two children in a small house in the quiet residential neighbourhood of Southmost. The young couple's oldest child is a healthy talkative three-year-old named Elizabeth. In a room at the back of the inexpensively furnished house, a new baby, two-month-old Stephanie, is asleep in her crib. In early 1991, Guadalupe was five months pregnant and went to have an ultrasound to find out whether she was going to have a boy or another girl. The test, however, indicated something else. Guadalupe's baby had anencephaly; it was not developing a brain. Guadalupe had an abortion that day.

At the time, it was simply a personal tragedy for the Esparzas. Within months, however, her unborn baby's condition had begun to fit into a horrifying and unusually widespread pattern of foetuses suffering from neural tube defects not only in Brownsville but all along the border.

The scare began when the infection-control nurse at Brownsville's Valley Regional Medical Center noticed that two pregnant women, one of them Guadalupe, had come in during the same 24-hour period in the month of March and were found to have anencephalic babies, even though it is a fairly rare birth defect. A month later, three more women came in with anencephalic babies in a 36-hour period. The cases were reported to the Texas Health Department, who in turn contacted the US Centers for Disease Control. By 1992 it had become apparent that Brownsville and the surrounding county's average for neural tube defects was almost 30 per 10,000 live births, three times the national average for Hispanics, and five times the national average for non-Hispanic whites.

Anencephaly and spina bifida, when the brain or the spinal cord of the foetus fails to develop, are both examples of neural tube defects. Another, when herniation of the nervous tissue occurs through a defect in the back of the skull, is known as encephalocele.

Doctors studying the phenomenon have long thought 'socioeconomic factors', namely poverty, to be the main cause of the condition. Cameron County, which is 82 per cent Hispanic and where 42 per cent of families live below the federal poverty line, would certainly seem to fit that description. Recent studies, however, have also linked neural tube defects to other conditions, such as the heavy use of alcohol during pregnancy or lack of folic acid in the diet. Supplements of folic acid to prevent cases of neural tube defects are now common and have shown positive results.

Yet almost instinctively, people in Brownsville and Matamoros turned towards the *maquiladoras* as the culprits, even though the leaching of pesticides from nearby market produce farms into the Río Grande - the area's main source of drinking water - could also be a factor. Says Dr Carmen Rocco, director of the Brownsville Community Health Center, who has been following the trend, 'These were all young women in good health. They were not a high-risk group. That's why we are looking at environmental causes. What else could it be?'

In July 1992 the Texas Department of Health and the Centers for Disease Control had published a joint report on the high incidence of neural tube defects, but found no conclusive evidence for their cause. Air and water quality tests had not found anything exceeding state limits on contamination. The report admitted, however, that 'environmental monitoring data ... is limited in quantity, scope, and to some extent, its utility to fully address concerns about the potential impact of environmental pollutants on the population.' It went on to suggest more testing and investigation.

Local environmentalists and health experts found the investigation flawed. 'Not everyone was interviewed, first of all,' says Domingo González of the Coalition for Justice in the Maquiladoras. 'Out of 66 cases, only 28 were interviewed, so you didn't get the right information from people. They didn't do any interviews in Matamoros, and when they refer to the higher rate of incidence among Hispanics, what do they mean by that? Black Hispanics from Cuba or the Dominican Republic, Hispanics of indigenous descent, or what?'

When the news came out about Brownsville, evidence emerged that such tragedies are common in other Mexican border cities. In a study completed in 1993, the federal Health Secretariat found that between 1988 and early 1992 there were a total of 89 cases of anencephaly in Ciudad Juárez, 69 in Reynosa, (including 1987) and 38 in Nuevo Laredo. A study in Tamaulipas showed that the city of Matamoros led the state in incidences of anencephalic births. Yet when the Secretariat first announced that it would investigate the Juárez cases, its director, Guillermo Barrios, added that he personally rejected the notion that exposure to toxic chemicals had anything to do with it.

Guadalupe, who got married at 17, knows little of such debates - whether it was something genetic, the environment, or simply an act of God. 'It can't be in the air,' she says, 'because then everybody would have it. Maybe it's the water, with all those *maquiladoras* over there in Mexico, right close to the river.' For her, the cause of that one case of ancephaly among three children is just a mystery. A mystery that still hurts. 'When I was in the hospital,' she says, 'I saw the baby but I didn't let my husband see it. When it comes up on the news I turn it off. And I always tell him, I didn't let you see her in the hospital, why see it now? Sometimes,' she adds, 'I remember everything, how she looked and everything, and I don't like it. I cried a lot, because it looked so horrible.'

In March 1993 the parents of 18 anencephalic babies in Brownsville filed suit in a Texas state court, charging 88 *maquiladoras* with negligence. Several companies, including General Motors, Zenith, AT&T, Magnatek and Trico were named in the suit, which claimed that the plaintiffs 'suffered injuries arising out of exposure to hazardous chemicals, hazardous wastes, hazardous hydrocarbons, similarly harmful organic or mineral substances and/or other similarly harmful substances placed into the local environment through negligent acts or omissions.'

❄   ❄   ❄   ❄   ❄

Both the Mexican government and the *maquila* industry claim to have the pollution problem under control. The PRI government keeps changing the name of its environment department - from SEDUE (Secretariat for Urban Development and Ecology) to SEDESOL (Secretariat for Social Development) - rotating the men in charge and slowly increasing their budget for the border. It currently stands at 40 per cent of the national total, but remains ineffectual in dealing with an increasingly critical problem.

In October 1991, for example, President Salinas announced that his government would spend US$460 million along the border just to build new sewage treatment plants, yet by mid-1993, only one, a joint effort between Laredo, Texas and Nuevo Laredo, Tamaulipas, was being built. Until November 1993, the head of SEDESOL was Luis Donaldo Colosio, a man who would become Salinas' hand-picked presidential candidate, only to be assassinated at a campaign rally in Tijuana in March 1994, many suspect by members of the PRI itself. In July 1992, however, already in the grooming phase for the presidency, Colosio travelled to Matamoros with great fanfare and closed eight *maquiladoras*, even though neither the SEDESOL offices in the city itself nor the state capital, Ciudad Victoria, had ever made similar moves. SEDESOL, however, allows companies found guilty of infractions to present them with a clean-up plan and pay a refundable bond. Within days, the *maquiladoras* had resumed production. The persistent severity of the problem became frighteningly apparent during parallel accord negotiations to NAFTA in 1993, when politicians and environmentalists estimated the cost of cleaning up the border area at between US$6.5 and US$10 billion.

In January 1992 Matamoros set up its own municipal environment department, but its head, Moises Sena, in an interview on pollution problems in the city, never even mentioned the complaints about air quality around Colonia Uniones. 'There is a problem with some companies, not all,' he stressed, 'disposing of toxic materials in the city drains, but it's not critical. It's under control.'

On paper, and for certain types of emissions, the Mexican government has environmental standards that resemble those of the Environment Protection Agency in the US. But those EPA standards have done little to diminish sulphur emissions that cause acid rain in Canada, or curb the manufacture and use of chlorofluorocarbons, or CFCs, which destroy the ozone layer. Nor have they done much to preserve the quality of rivers, wetlands or forests.

Even cursory scrutiny of Mexico's commitment to protecting its environment - or its people - from the ravages of industrial pollution reveals massive loopholes. One result is the environmental disaster that is Mexico City. A second is the *maquila* industry.

Maquila industry spokesmen say that they comply with rules and standards set by the government, sending all hazardous wastes back into the US for disposal as required of twin plants by Mexican law. In an interview printed in one south Texas newspaper, for example, Don Adams, general manager of one of the Kemet plants in Matamoros, said, 'Basically, I think the industry gets a bum rap for the government's ineptitude.' Adams added, 'I think there is some [dumping] going on, but the companies I know here are living up to every letter of the law.'

Similarly, Oakley Keller, environmental safety manager of the Trico plant in Matamoros, claimed that his company was bringing in new technology to reduce the production of hazardous metal-laced sludge from chrome plating from 75 tons in 1989 down to 46 tons in 1990. The company spends about US$150,000 every year to ship the sludge, as well as waste oil, back to the US, he added. 'It upsets me,' he said in a newspaper interview, 'that the *maquilas* are viewed the way we are. I think the image the public has is that we're trying to take advantage of Mexico.'

Such comments typify the tendency among *maquiladora* managers to admit that though there may be a slight problem, they themselves would never dream of throwing a drum of solvents down the drain or allow poison gas to escape from the plant. It is a tendency shared by local environment officials, all of them pro-business, PRI appointees. Someone is at fault, but not them.

At a May 1991 bi-national meeting in Juárez, where neatly dressed housewives from the Keep El Paso Beautiful Campaign discussed a recycling programme, Dr René Franco, director of the Juárez Municipal Environmental Affairs department, took time off to say, 'Sure there's stuff in the Río Grande that shouldn't be there. Are you going to tell me who's responsible for putting it there?'

Reality presents quite a different picture to that painted by government and industry. A publication on *maquiladoras* and toxics by the US trade union confederation, the AFL-CIO, for example, describes how Kemet only lowered water emission levels after years of public pressure, culminating with pressure on head office by church groups in the US. Following their suggestions, Kemet has also set up a health and safety commission, composed equally of management and labour representatives. But all kinds of independent testing, as well as personal accounts from hapless residents, proves that the pollution problem in Matamoros as a whole shows no signs of improvement. Hundreds of Mexican families still live near stinking drainage ditches, particularly noisome factories or illegal dump sites, while the figures from an increasing number of studies indicate the presence of noxious chemicals in the water, the air and the ground.

It is estimated that 100 million gallons of raw sewage containing pesticides, heavy metals and solvents is dumped into the Río Grande every day. In 1990 the Council on Scientific Affairs of the American Medical Association called the US-Mexico border region a virtual cesspool and a breeding ground for infectious diseases.

In the same year, a study by the National Toxics Campaign Fund, a Boston-based environmental group, found that water samples at 16 out of 22 factories violated quality standards. Chemicals such as xylenes - which can cause liver, lung, kidney and brain damage - and other toxics in some cases

1,000 times higher than EPA limits were found in lab tests in 100 separate water samples collected from discharge pipes at the 22 US-owned plants. In Matamoros, some samples contained acid ph levels so high they would burn the skin.

Some observers believe that smaller companies are more at fault than the big companies, which can afford to ship their wastes to the US for proper disposal or install anti-pollution equipment. But in the case of General Motors' Rimir plant, which makes car bumpers, the National Toxics Campaign Fund study turned up counts of xylene of 2,800 parts per million, ethyl benzene at 430 ppm, as well as acetone, methylene chloride and tolene. The EPA's cumulative permissible standard for all toxic organic chemicals is just 2.13 ppm. Rimir officials responded that their own studies had found much lower counts, within the permissible standard.

The following April, after environmental groups publicly condemned General Motors, Mexican inspectors temporarily shut down Rimir. Soon afterwards, General Motors announced that, where necesssary, it would refit all its plants with the kind of pollution abatement equipment that has been the law in the US since 1972, almost 20 years before the Boston study was made.

In Tijuana, independent tests by the *Los Angeles Times* in 1991 found all kinds of chemicals in water samples taken from drainage pipes in the city's industrial parks and residential neighbourhoods. One sample contained mercury at levels five times the maximum US standard. Other tests found high levels of methylene chloride, a carcinogen, as well as excessive readings of 1,1,1 trichloroethane, which can damage the heart, liver, and nervous system.

Earlier EPA tests of Tijuana sewage carried out in April 1990 found both solvents and heavy metals, including lead, a highly toxic substance which attacks the brain and nervous system, 100 times higher that the allowable US maximum. It is estimated that 12 million gallons of sewage is now dumped annually into the Tía Juana River, which flows up through the city before crossing the border into California. The resulting pollution is so bad that the river's mouth, Imperial Beach, has had to be closed as a health hazard. In 1991 California state authorities declared a state of emergency in the Tijuana River Valley because of the severe health threat posed by the levels of pathogens in the residential sewage.

The *Times* study also found two suspected carcinogens at 18 to 24 times acceptable US levels in samples taken from drains near furniture factories. Both of the chemicals detected are used in furniture manufacturing. A report by the Washington-based General Accounting Office, an investigative arm of the US Congress, found that 78 per cent of California furniture manufacturers relocating to Mexico did so because state pollution laws were too stringent. One of those laws would have required them to switch from cheaper solvent-based varnishes, such as those found in Tijuana, to water-based varnishes by 1996.

The number of people employed in California furniture manufacturing fell from 85,000 in 1987 to 55,000 in 1991. Predictions held that a further 125,000 jobs in metal-finishing would also be lost, as well as those in other industries generating large amounts of toxic waste. Pollution control does not come cheap. A December 1990 EPA study estimated that 'total annualised costs for all pollution control activities in the US' were running at US$115 billion that year. With the law fully implemented, these would rise to US$185 billion by the year 2000. That figure represents 2.8 per cent of the country's predicted GDP, up from 2.1 per cent in 1990 and 0.9 per cent in 1972.

In Mexicali, studies of the Río Nuevo carried out yearly by the California Regional Water Quality Control Board have found 100 different industrial chemicals, along with 15 viruses capable of causing dysentery, cholera, typhoid, meningitis and hepatitis. This river flows north into the Salton Sea in California, where state officials acknowledge that it is the filthiest waterway in the state.

In Nogales, Sonora, up to 30 million gallons of untreated sewage, or 'black waters,' as they are called in Spanish, flow through the Nogales Arroyo into Arizona, where it is then treated in the American city's sanitation plant. Carcinogenic solvents, as well as chromium, lead, manganese, cadmium, arsenic and mercury have been found even in underground aquifers unconnected to the Nogales Arroyo, that are used for drinking water.

According to a recent study by Roberto Sánchez of the Northern Border College in Tijuana and by the University of Arizona, at least 10 per cent and possibly 24 per cent of Nogales' drinking water is contaminated, especially those wells nearest the *maquiladoras*. Samples from 22 wells in Mexico and 13 in Arizona, as well as city sewers, found 'very, very high' incidences, says Sánchez, of chlorinated solvents and bacterial contamination. The samples were tested in two independent labs to verify the results.

In spite of the evidence of sewage and industrial solvent contamination at five times the acceptable levels, water from one such contaminated source, a privately-owned well called La Tomatera, is pumped into trucks and sold to poor *colonia* residents in Nogales. The government closed the well when presented with the test results, but after just three days, it quietly reopened and has been in business ever since. According to Sánchez, 'The poorest people with no mains water supply pay three to four times as much for water from the trucks that is of poor quality and polluted - so they suffer economically and physically.' The majority of *maquiladora* and other workers living in Nogales' poorly serviced and outlying districts have to buy their water from trucks.

In Ciudad Juárez, the burgeoning population of the city produces 22 million gallons of sewage daily, yet does not have access to even one sewage treatment plant. While no testing has been done, companies are likely to be dumping toxic wastes into the same sewage system. Dr Irene Cech, a professor of environmental science and hydrology at the University of Texas Health Science Center in Houston, says that a study of some of the hundreds of wells drilled to meet drinking water needs in Juárez revealed contamination from bacterial pollution which had leached through the porous soil from drainage ditches. Blaming a combination of poor living conditions, faecal pollution and *maquiladora* waste, she has also found frightening health statistics. Gall bladder and liver cancer are higher in the 33 Texas counties that get their water from the Río Grande than the national average. In border counties between El Paso and Brownsville, the incidence of hepatitis is six times the US average.

Even the Juárez Environment Department's Dr Franco has admitted that waste water goes into a canal which is then used for irrigating crops. In Agua Prieta, Sonora, about four hours away from Juárez, a similar tendency was noted by a member of an environmental group there. 'Companies throw toxic wastes down the drains,' says Miguel Angel González, 'it goes into the Agua Prieta arroyo, the water is used for irrigating and people eventually consume the produce, whether it's vegetables or meat from cattle that eat the grass. It's not a long cycle.'

Dangerous waste is not only being released into the waterways and air. Dumping by the *maquiladoras* of toxic and other wastes in landfill sites is poisoning both soil and water. Companies also store hazardous chemicals inside factory premises which sometimes border populated neighbourhoods. According to a 1988 study by the Northern Border College, 'Many companies have been storing dangerous chemicals in drums inside their assembly plants, and once they run out of space, they get rid of these containers in clandestine disposal sites.' Sánchez has pointed out that there are only eight licensed disposal sites for industrial wastes in the whole of Mexico.

In March 1988 an article in the *Brownsville Herald* exposed the dumping in Matamoros of toxic waste in the Gato Negro landfill site, only about two miles away from the city's most popular beach. SEDUE had authorised the use of the site for non-toxic wastes from some of the industrial plants, such as General Motors' Rimir, as well as its Componentes Mecánicos *maquiladora* which manufactures vinyl dashboards and high pressure hoses. The industrial wastes of Parker Hannifin, which makes rubber products, have also been found on the banks of the Río Grande. An American manager for the International Water and Boundary Commission reported seeing mountains of plastic and other debris with the company's name at a site about four miles from the National Audubon Society's Sabal Palm Sanctuary. The company protested that it had hired a private Mexican contractor to dispose of its rubbish and didn't know that it was ending up in the river. Parker Hannifin duly pledged to clean up the site, but days later the heaps of plastic were mysteriously set on fire. The authorities said that the fire had been deliberately set, with palm branches having been used to broom over footprints.

Outside Reynosa there is a huge dump containing plastic, metals, rubber and factory sludge. A brief walk around its perimeter reveals barrels and cardboard boxes with all kinds of company names, such as Zenith, which claims that the waste disposed of there is not toxic. Nearby is a black lake of rust-tinted oily water in an old caliche quarry. Similar to limestone, the caliche is highly porous and all kinds of toxins could leach into surrounding soil and groundwater. The companies claim that the site is licensed. Mexican enviromental and municipal officals disagree, but have done nothing to clean up the mess.

In Nogales, explosions of gas from the municipal dump have often forced the evacuation of students from a nearby school. In Mexicali, a dumpsite used by a recycling company called MEXACO was found to contain more than 7,000 barrels of toxic waste from 27 local plants, as well as 60 more in nearby Tijuana. By October 1992, SEDESOL had promised to close down the site, as well as the disposal company, and to jail the MEXACO manager. The company and various of its clients offered to clean up the site, but as of May 1993 they had received yet another extension from the government on the deadline to complete the work.

In Tijuana a few years ago, environmental officials and army staff closed 60 illegal dumps. Ecologists say that since then, with an estimated 1,500 metric tons of industrial waste produced in the city daily, such sites have only proliferated. Private Mexican waste disposal companies, of which there are about a dozen in the city, make a fortune from the business. Some, such as Hércules, which has 400 commercial and industrial clients and collects 200 metric tons of garbage a day, donate money to local political parties as insurance against their dumps being closed down. 'The industrial waste and residues generated by hundreds of *maquiladora* and manufacturing plants have gone to rest for years, without any control, in clandestine dump sites,' said a January 1992 article in the Mexican weekly magazine, *Proceso*. Five dump fires had taken place just in the final months of 1991, the article claimed. SEDUE officials discovered illegally disposed-of industrial waste in one such site, two square kilometres in area, in September 1991. They that said it constituted a public danger, especially for the 400 people who earn a living picking through the garbage for recyclable material. In 1992 officials were apprised by local residents of two more sites, one in a district called Jardines de la Mesa, with at least

800 barrels of toxic waste, and another, abandoned by Los Angeles-based Alco Pacific, 15 kilometres outside of Tijuana on the road to Tecate.

Alco Pacific extracts lead from used car batteries, and ships the ingots back to the US for sale. Until March 1992 the company had never been inspected by health or environment officials, in spite of the extremely dangerous nature of its business. After 11 years, when the inspectors finally did show up, they found a toxic horror story - 80,000 tons of lead sulphate spread out in large mounds over the dump site, toxic and explosive chemicals stored in open drums, and battery acid, dumped onto the ground for years, fueling a continuously burning underground fire. Near the now-abandoned plant, residents of a small, semi-rural community called El Florido had been putting up for years with dust-laden air, as well as respiratory and other illnesses.

The site is currently being cleaned up at a cost of US$20 million to the Mexican tax payer, money that could have been used to improve schools, build clinics or replace shacks with decent housing. Alco Pacific has been charged in the US, however, in a landmark case which saw the company that hired them to dismantle the batteries, RSR-Quemetco, fined US$2.5 million in 1993. The firm pleaded no contest to felony charges.

The budget to deal with such problems certainly increased in Mexico in the early 1990s, as the Salinas government struggled to improve its environmental image during Free Trade negotiations. In 1989, public expenditure on the environment amounted to just US$6.6 million. It rose to US$11.7 million in 1990, US$38.4 million in 1991, and to US$78 million in 1992, a figure still well below the US$100 million budgeted for promoting and lobbying for NAFTA in 1991. Despite repeated requests, SEDESOL officials say they cannot find their 1993 budget, but claim that overall government spending on the environment stands at 2.5 billion. That figure however remains a dubious one, since it includes such items as road-paving, oil refining and social improvement projects for the poor.

Private firms meanwhile spent an estimated US$4 billion in 1993 on environmental studies, pollution control devices, water sanitation plants and other technology. Yet the head of the Mexican Ecological Movement says that only one per cent of Mexican companies are spending enough to stop pollution.

SEDESOL officials add that in 1992, 672 plant inspections took place among the border's 2,000 *maquiladoras*, resulting in only 17 total closures. They also admit that although they would probably need at least 2,000 inspectors just for Mexico City, only 200 were trained in 1992 for all of Mexico.

Another problem is Mexican law, which on paper seemingly insists that toxic waste products from the processing of imported materials be returned to the country of origin. But the law allows *maquiladoras* to 'donate' their toxic waste to charities for recycling. SEDESOL currently estimates that over half of the country's twin plants produce some kind of toxic chemical in their processing, yet only a third of those can prove that they send it back to the US.

One example of the Mexican government's inability or unwillingness to clean up its border area sits just a few kilometres outside Matamoros on the highway to Reynosa. With its rows of white tanks and miles of winding pipes and tubes, striped towers and metal ladders, the huge Química Fluor plant spreads over the semi-tropical landscape. According to the company brochure, the factory property covers 150 hectares. What the brochure does not describe, however, is the huge pile of greyish-white calcium sulphate that covers much of that land.

Originally built in 1971, the plant belongs to a consortium made up of Wilmington, Delaware-based E.I. DuPont Corp, with 33 per cent of the shares, and Empresas Frisco, a Mexican mining firm within the powerful Grupo Carso consortium. One of Mexico's largest holdings, Grupo Carso belongs to Carlos Slim Helu, a close friend of President Salinas.

Química Fluor is one of the largest hydrofluoric acid processing plants in the world, churning out 70,000 tons of the substance a year. Ninety-eight per cent of it is exported to the US and Latin America; the rest is bought by PEMEX. Mexico can manufacture the product relatively cheaply; it has one of the three largest deposits of fluorite in the world and the sixth largest sulphur reserves.

In 1980, two workers at Química Fluor were killed and five others injured during an acid leak in the factory. A cloud formed and floated over the city. Three thousand local residents had to be evacuated.

But a further problem results from the byproduct of the process, the chalky white substance that sits by the ton outside the plant. Since 1981, the company has been donating almost 200,000 tons of this material every year to the municipality of Matamoros, to be used as a base for roads and streets. A DuPont representative in Mexico says that although the calcium is not dangerous, merely irritating, it should be paved over or covered. But the municipality, after receiving it free from the company, sells it to householders in the *colonias* to cover up muddy streets and lanes, usually at about US$20 or US$25 per load. Secondly they don't pave it, since no-one has thought to donate free tarmac. The resulting layers of calcium sulphate have proven to be extremely irritating. Although DuPont says that the product is inert and cannot cause burns to skin or eyes, people in Matamoros have been complaining about irritations to their skin and eyes when it is windy and the air full of dust. Some scientists have said that calcium sulphate, being a pure alkali, could damage membranes in the human body, especially in the eyes and nose.

Across the highway from Química Fluor are several houses belonging to people who farm a piece of *ejido* land, farm plots which up until 1992, the farmer could pass on to family but not sell. A few miles up the highway is another *ejido*, home to about 3,000 people. In all, an estimated 10,000 people live on *ejidos* near the Química Fluor plant.

The *colonia* across the highway from the plant is called Las Rusias, and the powdery calcium blows across its residents' homes and land. 'The company is a danger because it is so close to the city and our land,' says farmer Erasmo Lucio Garza, 49, who cultivates sorghum, corn, and beans on his ten hectares. 'The powder blows onto our crops and into the irrigation canal. Even here in the house it really bothers my eyes. Everyone complains about it.' Química Fluor offered factory jobs to some of the young men on the *ejido*, but according to Mr Garza, no-one wants to take up the offer. 'We can't tolerate this situation any more,' he says. A few years ago, he adds, 'I went to a protest demonstration in Ciudad Victoria, but the authorities there just told us that we were a group of liars and agitators.'

Up until 1983 Química Fluor paid compensation to local farmers for crop damage, but according to DuPont spokeman, Joaquín Carmona, the company then carried out new tests on the problem. 'The company conducted studies together with SEDUE and the Department of Agriculture,' says Carmona, 'reviewing all of the farming practices, and found that the problem was that the land was very poor, with a high salinity level. And also, not all of the peasants practice the proper farming methods.' The company now claims that there are no problems with calcium sulphate, and since the study was completed, has stopped the compensation payments.

In 1990, the *ejido* farmers pressured SEDUE to study the emissions from Química Fluor again, complaining that their land was still being contaminated. According to an agronomist who had independently looked at the *ejido* farmers' problems, even two parts per million of soluble fluoride was dangerous to health, yet the mountain of waste outside the plant contained levels of more than 750 ppm. He added that the powder was also the cause of many chronic eye and throat problems among *ejido* residents.

Despite the installation of US$15 million worth of pollution abatement equipment in 1985, people in Matamoros are also worried about low-level emissions of the acid gas itself. Farmers at Ejido Guadalupe, about four kilometres northwest of Química Fluor, believe they are losing about three-quarters of their crops. 'The government says we're not losing it because of the fluoride,' says one farmer, 'that it's bad management by the farmers or that the earth has a lot of salt in it. But I think the government is trying to protect the company.'

Thirty-seven vegetation samples analysed in 1986 by Dr Lourdes de Bauer of the Autonomous University of Chapingo, near Mexico City, did indeed reveal fluoride levels exceeding 40 ppm in leafy plants, 25 ppm in a mesquite bush, and 120 ppm in sorghum. A year earlier, a Department of Agriculture study found counts of 440 ppm in plants from Ejido Las Rusias. Química Fluor claimed that the study was flawed.

In January 1991, an executive decree signed by President Salinas established a so-called 'Ecological Belt' two kilometres wide around the plant, banning any new settlement inside the belt. Local farmers are afraid that the government could also use the decree as a first step to expelling them from their land and expropriating it for the company. More insidious still, the decree releases Química Fluor from any liability for deaths or injuries from any kind of accident such as a gas leak like the one that occurred in Bhopal, India, in 1985, leaving almost 3,000 dead. In the Química Fluor case, such a disaster would not constitute grounds for lawsuits against the company.

The decree has angered many Matamoros residents, who see it as yet another favour from the nation's president to a close personal friend, at enormous potential expense to their lives. They insist that they want the company to relocate as far away from them as possible.

❋ ❋ ❋ ❋ ❋

As the harm to Mexicans and their environment grows worse, and government officials do little or nothing, the numbers of angry people are growing. In June 1991, 3,000 Matamoros *colonia* dwellers occupied the international bridge spanning the Río Grande between their city and Brownsville. According to Teresa Méndez, both police and environment officials furiously threatened to throw the leaders, including herself, in jail. Groups have protested in front of the factories themselves, demanding to see the managers. Several of Teresa's angry neighbours even went up to New York to protest when the United Nations took the bizarre move of awarding Salinas a special 'Earth Prize', honouring his environmental accomplishments.

In 1992, residents of Playas de Tijuana, a suburb on the Pacific coast, successfully mobilised to stop an American company called Chemical Waste Management from constructing a toxic waste incinerator there. In less than a year, the government backed down on giving the company building permission, but has instead awarded a permit for somewhere else in Mexico. At the end of 1992, the residents of Colonia Uniones scored a victory of sorts when the Retzloff plant finally closed down. Although she acknowledged the plant probably closed for economic reasons, Teresa believes, 'we may have had a little to do with it. Isn't it great that it's gone! Now there is one less to make our lives miserable.'

'What we want,' she adds, 'what we're fighting for is to have all these plants simply move somewhere else, let them go somewhere where there are no houses. They should be in the industrial parks, not neighbourhoods.

We were living here first. Why should we be the ones to go? Who will build us new houses?'

Some North American ecologists support the Free Trade Agreement signed by Mexico, Canada and the US in 1992, despite fears that environmental damage caused by the unregulated growth of *maquiladoras* could prove merely a taste of the future under NAFTA. With the parallel accords added to NAFTA by the Clinton Administration, companies in all three nations will be subject to fines and exemption from the tariff reductions if it can be proved that they knowingly harmed the environment. A similar accord exists for labour issues.

The problem remains that while even today laws in Mexico prohibit pollution, they are all too easily circumvented. Such a long-standing tradition is unlikely to be ended by an unwieldy tri-lateral commission. While some environmentalists maintain that the additional income generated by NAFTA will enable Mexico to develop economically and spend more money on the environment, they fail to see that in the US, itself the wealthiest nation on earth, thousands of environmental crimes continue to be committed every day. They are also ignoring that more than 25 years of industrial development along the border is the cause, not the solution to the hundreds of serious problems that plague the area.

Teresa Méndez believes there is modern technology that these plants could be installing to deal with the smell, the leaks, and the toxic waste. Companies, on the other hand, like to claim that inside the factories themselves, workers do not get sick, throw up or complain of headaches. As far as Teresa is concerned, these companies don't want to have to spend the money. They see dealing with the emission problems as just too expensive.

Teresa and her group would rather their poisonous neighbours simply moved away. 'Everyone in the *colonias* is taking the position that we're not the ones who are going,' she says, 'we are very united on that. We've been fighting these companies for ten years and will keep on fighting them.'

5

Handle with Care

Health and Safety in the Factories

The director of the Matamoros School for Special Education, Isabel de la O Alonso, first began to notice them in 1982. Dr de la O worked with about 200 youngsters with physical and mental handicaps, the majority of them children of working class parents. But one small group stood out. Their disabilities ranged from severe retardation to slow learning. Physically they bore similar characteristics, such as broad noses, thin lips, bushy eyebrows, and webbed hands and feet. A few were deaf. Yet the children did not fit any of the categories of birth defects that she had previously studied or observed. Dr de la O decided to compile a clinical history and soon found that all the children had one thing in common - their mothers, while pregnant, had worked in the same Matamoros *maquiladora*. It had been called Mallory Capacitors, and the children became known as the Mallory Children.

The Mallory workers had to handle a range of toxic chemicals in the plant, but one in particular seemed the most likely cause for such severe birth defects. The capacitors - small devices for television sets which store an electrical charge - were washed in a product the workers only knew as '*electrolito.*' Dr de la O believes that this liquid might well have contained PCBs, as her research indicated some similarities in the women's descriptions of the effects of the fluid and studies already carried out in the US. PCBs, or polychlorinated biphenyls, have been banned in the US because of their links to cancer. They are also believed to affect the body's chromosomes. The women recalled that working with '*electrolito*' caused their finger nails to turn black, a classic reaction to PCB exposure.

They are growing up now, leaving their teenage years and entering young adulthood, but they will always be the Mallory Children. Together they represent the most obvious legacy of the perilous conditions under which thousands of Mexicans toil for their minimum wage.

All along the border, they solder, glue, dip and wash parts in hundreds of liquids and chemicals with long, complicated names and dangerous side effects. They put up with skin rashes, burning eyes and sore throats. They work long hours without gloves, masks, or in many cases, proper ventilation. Aside from the low wages, another compelling attraction for setting up a *maquiladora* in Mexico are the minimal health and safety standards. Mexico has one of the highest industrial accident and illness rates in the world, according to the International Labour Organisation, with 23 cases per 100,000 workers annually between 1987 and 1991. According to the IMSS, that rate rose by 6 per cent between 1988 and 1992. Yet if Mexican workers voice any protest about these conditions, they risk losing their jobs.

One Mallory Child discovered by Dr de la O is the son of a barber, Juan Zamala, who rents the bottom floor of her parents' Matamoros home. Francisco Javier Zamala Duenes is now 17. He spends most of his time on the smooth tile floor of his parents' peach-coloured stucco house in Colonia San Rafael, waving an old leather belt back and forth in an endless configuration of invisible patterns. 'That's his daily occupation,' says his mother, Irma, grimly. He also likes to play with water and listen to music. Sometimes Francisco goes outside and sits by the iron bar fence, but children from a nearby school taunt him.

Francisco only began to walk at 12, says Irma. A lean-limbed teenager with large joints, dark hair trimmed short, he sleeps during the day, and is awake all night, so the family always leave the lights and the radio on for him. Looking after him has never been easy. 'He had to teach me how,' she explains. 'When he wants a drink of water, he goes and gets a cup or goes to the sink. That means I have to get it for him. When he's hungry, he gets some food and puts it in my hand. That means I have to feed him.'

Irma got the job at Mallory in 1971 and worked there for five years before being laid off when the company did away with its afternoon shift. With four children, the family needed the extra money. It was the only job she's ever had and because of it, her youngest son will need constant care for the rest of his life.

Irma worked in different departments in the factory, including quality control. She claims that her only contact with the liquid believed to contain PCBs came when she had to impregnate a cap with cotton soaked in the liquid, which sometimes spattered onto her face and hands. 'Every night I used to finish the shift at the end of my tether,' she recalls, 'absolutely exhausted. People fainted there all the time, so much that the people at the IMSS clinic said we must be faking it, that we had to be exaggerating. Also it smelled bad. I remember that when they opened the factory gates that terrible smell would come out to meet us as we went in to our shift.'

When Francisco was born, remembers Irma, 'he was *muy chiquitito*, very small, and had to be left in an incubator for a while.' When he was a month old, she noticed that he couldn't see properly. 'I took him to the IMSS and they told me that he had an incurable illness. So I started going to a specialist in Reynosa, and there they put electrical things on his head and did various tests. That's when they told me that his brain wasn't normal.'

At first Irma blamed herself for having Francisco when she was 36 years old. 'But now I know that other girls, young newlyweds who worked there and got pregnant, had kids like mine,' she says.

The firm that owned the *maquiladora*, P.R. Mallory, became the property of a company called Dart Industries in a corporate takeover in 1977. By then the Matamoros plant had been closed down. Dart then merged with another American firm called Kraft Company. Mallory currently belongs to Kraft, as a subsidiary of their Duracell International division, a battery manufacturer. While the *maquiladora* was operating they ran two shifts of 300 workers. Thousands of women passed through their doors. 'It is almost impossible to calculate how many children were born affected by the chemicals their mothers were handling at Mallory,' claims Dr de la O. 'The effects are very varied. The results range from the condition of someone like Francisco Javier, to someone who's just never done very well at school and will only ever be able to carry out the simplest unskilled labour.'

Ever since she found out the real cause of her son's birth defect, Irma Zamala has felt her resentment growing. 'What do I feel about it? Well, I feel very sad,' she says. 'I say that they had to have known that this could happen, or why else did they leave the US to come down here? When children are born like this it's because they were poisoning us. I feel very bad about the whole thing. You only go out and get a job because you need the money for your family.'

Fifteen years after Dr de la O discovered the first Mallory Children, a lawyer in Brownsville decided to seek justice for them. Richard Palmer had just moved to Brownsville and opened his practice when a woman came to his office. 'She said that she had been trying to have her case heard for 12 years,' recounts paralegal Sheri Kenner, 'and that it wouldn't surprise her if he turned her down as well. But he was her last hope. So we began doing some investigating and found that we'd really opened a can of worms.' When the union in Matamoros refused to co-operate by giving them the names of former Mallory employees from their records, Palmer began putting advertisements in the local papers. Soon he had over one hundred families listed as plaintiffs, all of whom had worked for years at Mallory, all of them with handicapped children. In 1992 court dates were set for the trial to start in 1994. All through 1993, the office took depositions from people who had worked at Mallory, amassing 77 by April. Palmer is suing Duracell Batteries, which denies all involvement. But according to Kenner, Mallory merely changed their name to Duracell, which is still responsible for what happened in the Matamoros plant.

✲ ✲ ✲ ✲ ✲

Few independent studies or reports on occupational hazards in the *maquiladoras* exist. Workplace accidents occur all the time in every country as thousands of commodities are produced, packaged and sent off for distribution. Yet by the standards of countries like Britain, Canada or the US, Mexican workers are woefully unprotected. Interviews with dozens of workers along the border show that the daily accidents, the polluted air, the smell of fumes, the heat and noise all contribute to the growing dissatisfaction in the plants.

The IMSS runs a scheme for workers injured in the workplace. If an accident occurs, the worker goes to a doctor at the IMSS, has a paper signed by the company, and receives his salary from the state while off work. For their employee's membership in the system, companies pay a premium to the Mexican government which goes up with the number of accidents at the plant. Many companies therefore try to keep their accident rates down as much as possible. In some cases they install safety measures and carry out training procedures, but in many others they simply refuse to acknowledge that the accident was the company's fault.

If a worker sues their employer for damages, the case can spend years in legal proceedings. Furthermore, the federal labour law sets out a table of damages owed workers for loss of limbs or serious injury. According to labour lawyers, should negligence be proved, the maximum pension owed to families of workers who are killed on the job, is an automatic 723 days worth of the minimum wage. At the current minimum wage, this amounts to some US$3,615, with correspondingly less awarded for the loss of an arm or hand.

Mexico's medical system leaves many loopholes. In July 1989, a car parts plant worker named Alfonso Marmolejo, a client of Juárez lawyer Gustavo de la la Rosa, slipped on a greasy floor in Ford's Favesa factory one day in July 1989 where he had been working for two years, and severely injured his back. IMSS paid for his medical expenses and rehabilitation, but he was left partially disabled. As a result, he was unable to carry out his normal duties at the plant, which refused to offer him an alternative job. 'I was told that with my slower movements now, I'm too much of a risk,' says Marmolejo.

Besides the accidents, there is widespread unprotected use of a whole series of toxic materials involved in the manufacturing process. In electronics, plastics, furniture manufacturing and a host of other industries, poisonous substances are used for painting, glueing, cleaning, removing grease or as a base for soldering. According to Roberto Sánchez of the Northern Border College in Tijuana, 'The solvents most commonly used in industries like electronics are unfortunately the types of substances with the greatest risk to both the environment and workers' health.' In the Erika plant in Reynosa, for example, which makes intravenous bags for hospitals for the Chicago-based W.R. Grace Co., the fumes from the adhesives are so strong that workers frequently faint.

Another danger is the use of molten metals in soldering, dipping, and electroplating. In the Los Angeles-based Magnatek factory in Matamoros, workers dip light bulbs into molten material containing lead, without masks or other protective gear. Elsewhere along the border, explosions, gas escapes and leaks of toxic fumes send hundreds at a time to hospital. Commenting on a 1991 study of occupational health impacts of *maquiladoras* in Matamoros and Reynosa, University of Lowell professor, Rafael Moure-Eraso, wrote, 'The survey found clear evidence that *maquiladora* workers are suffering from musculoskeletal disorders related to working conditions, including rapid pace of work, poor workplace design and other ergonomic hazards. Acute health effects compatible with chemical exposures were also identified, indicating the potential for the future development of chronic diseases in the workforce.'

Studies carried out by Catalina Denman of the Colegio de Sonora in Hermosillo show that women working in *maquiladoras* are nearly three times more likely to give birth to underweight babies than women working in services or commerce. Low birth weight is one of the most accurate indicators of the general state of health of the child, according to Denman. In 1985, Denman also discovered that although women in Nogales between the ages of 15 and 44 constituted only 26 per cent of those insured at the IMSS, they accounted for 78 per cent of hospital cases that year. Denman believes that factors behind such statistics include long work days, uncomfortable working positions, stress and exposure to toxins.

Along the length of the border, according to Denman, half of the cases registered at the local IMSS 'are conditioned on risks inside the factories. One observes high rates of problems of sight, dermatitis, renal, muscular and circulatory problems, as well as frequent accidents [affecting] fingernails, fingers, hands and feet. Although there are no statistics that measure the impact of stress among women *maquiladora* workers, the frequency with which cases of massive hysteria are reported demands that this be considered a serious problem in worker health.'

A booklet of recent press clippings published by the US-based Coalition for Justice in the Maquiladoras reveals a swathe of incidents including lethal accidents, even though the clippings only cover the cities of Matamoros and Reynosa. In many cases, factory security personnel have actually impeded workers from leaving or authorities from entering the plants to investigate accidents.

In January 1989 nine workers in the Idacon textile plant in Matamoros were overcome by phenol gas fumes seeping out of the nearby Preservation Products plant. Idacon plant managers assured the press that the phenol gas was not toxic, merely irritating, yet Preservation Products manufactures pentachlorophenol, a wood preservative linked to cancer, birth defects, weakening of the immune system and blood, liver and skin diseases.

Five months later, also in Matamoros, Enrique Ramírez was electrocuted and killed in the Parker Hannifin O-Ring plant, after being sent to connect wires from one machine to another. Because it was raining and the roof was leaking, Ramírez reportedly asked his supervisor if he could cut the power to the machines first. The supervisor refused. The company paid the Ramírez family US$1,500 compensation for his death.

Four weeks later, 36 workers from the Trico Corp windscreen wiper component plant in Matamoros were taken to hospital with severe symptoms of poisoning, reportedly from natural gas. Later, another 176 workers in the plant complained of feeling sick from the same leak, but since the plant security system did not register a second escape, manager Jorge Pena said that their complaints were merely the results of 'auto-suggestion'.

In May 1990, a motor exploded and set fire to the General Motors Deltronicos plant in Matamoros, which manufactures car radios. According to newspaper reports, during and after the fire, plant security guards prevented the entry into the plant of both firemen and ambulance personnel. Some 70 employees, mostly women between the ages of 17 and 22, were overcome with smoke and had to be hospitalised. The panicking workers originally ran outside when the fire started, but were ordered back to their posts once the fire was put out and told to resume production.

The following September, 20 women workers at the CMI ceramic insulators plant in Matamoros were taken to hospital after an early morning leak of ethyl alcohol.

In the early 1980s, 27-year-old chemical engineer José Herebia died while working at General Motors' Rimir plant. Herebia was inspecting a chemical storage tank when he noticed toxic gases. He tried to get out of the tank, but slipped on the narrow metal ladder, losing his mask, and fell. Plant supervisors prevented the press from entering the plant after the accident.

In October 1993, two workers were killed and five injured when an explosion, believed to have been caused by a mix of solvents and glue in an unventilated area, tore through a Tijuana *maquiladora* making picture frames. The area around the plant is heavily populated and had to be evacuated because of the fire.

Accident victims often complain that the companies will not let them leave. Apolonia Resendiz, 45, lives in a modest neighbourhood in the town of Río Bravo, midway between Matamoros and Reynosa. Her husband is a truck driver and for the past ten years Apolonia has worked in Reynosa's largest Zenith plant, #13, where the strike broke out in 1984. She brings home just under US$30 a week from Zenith, after US$9 has been taken off for INFONAVIT housing and US$7 for transport to and from work. 'It seems like so little for a week's work that I've been doing a lot of overtime,' she adds. 'It's true you don't get much time to sleep, but at least I'm not like some of the young people there who drink Coke with diet pills to stay awake.'

In 1989, Apolonia was moved to a different section of the plant for a day where she had to solder fine copper wires. While looking for a free soldering stand, she knocked over a pot of hot glue onto her foot. She was only wearing tennis shoes and the cotton material and the glue began to fuse to her foot. A fellow worker tore off the burning shoe, leaving her with a deep and nasty burn. Three years later, her foot is still badly scarred. 'But the company wouldn't let me go to the IMSS,' recalls Apolonia, 'and the medical attention at Zenith has always been awful, even though the law says I have the right to go to a proper doctor.'

Apolonia also remembers two serious gas leaks at Zenith. The first one occurred in 1986 when a 50-gallon trichloroethane storage tank exploded and sent 100 workers to hospital. Trichloroethane is used to coat microchips and other electronic parts. 'People were fainting, dropping like flies,' she recalls. 'It was a terrible experience. The worst thing was that the guards wouldn't let people leave; we were all just in a mad rush to get out and get some fresh air. But they said no, the company rules are that you can't leave the plant.' In the end, she says, the panicking workers just shoved the guards aside. 'You'd think with a big company like that,' she adds, 'they'd be better organised for this kind of thing or not let it happen in the first place.' In the ten years she has been there, she says, the workforce has never been provided with accident training of any kind. Another accident occurred at Zenith in 1990, when six women, two of them pregnant, were overcome by fumes when the furnace where transistors are fired overheated and exploded.

Now Apolonia says the worst problem is the soldering areas. 'The smoke,' she says, 'burns your eyes and smells bad. In 1990 we demanded that they put in extractors. They said no for a long time, said we had to write up a memo and everything, then we said we'd call a work stoppage if they didn't put them in, so finally they did. Now there are extractors on some of the lines and not on others, but you do need a lot of them because if you're near a soldering stand the fumes really hit you.'

❋   ❋   ❋   ❋   ❋

María Concepción Ovalle, 25, works in a *maquila* called General de Cable, in the small city of Piedras Negras, Coahuila, across the Río Grande from Eagle Pass, Texas. She is a pretty young woman with a sense of humour remarkably intact despite the long years of hard work which began when she was just a teenager. Apologising for the mess in the rented two-room house she shares with her husband, Carlos, she admits, 'By the time I get home from work and picking up my son at the daycare centre, it's already about 8 o'clock. I make dinner and by nine, all I can do is fall into bed.'

Conchi, as her friends call her, grew up on a *ranchito*, a small farm near León, in the state of Guanajuato. Aged 14, she moved to the city of Torreón where she worked as a maid. At 15, she got her first industrial job, in a Torreón furniture factory. A year later, in 1983, she moved north to the border with a friend who had said, 'Let's go up to Piedras Negras, because there is plenty of work up there and good wages.' Now married with two children, one staying with her mother down in Guanajuato, Conchi knows that life on the border is no picnic.

At General de Cable, Conchi spends nine hours a day cutting and soldering cable. One day in June 1992, she needed to cut the lining off a piece of cable and couldn't find the right tool. She asked a supervisor for the tool, but was told just to use a razor. She did so and ended up badly cutting her finger. A foreman told her to go to the IMSS but the same supervisor, (the cousin of the plant manager, according to Conchi), told her to see the secretary, since the plant had no nurse. The secretary swabbed the finger with alcohol and put some tissue around it, and told Conchi that she would waste a lot of time if she left and went off to the hospital. But the finger, missing quite a bit of flesh, continued to give her a great deal of pain, and Conchi decided to go to the IMSS anyway. There a doctor treated the cut, and told her to take three days off. Later he told her to take off another 14 days because the cut was not healing.

When Conchi went to the plant to get a standard form signed recognising the accident, she was surprised to see that the supervisor had written that the accident was due to Conchi's negligence. He claimed that she had not obeyed company rules, carried out a task that was not hers to do, using the wrong tool, and thus caused the accident. Even the IMSS doctor commented that the excuse given on the form was ridiculous, but by not admitting that the accident was work-related, the company avoided paying Conchi for her time off and averted a slight increase in insurance premiums to the IMSS. Returning to work, Conchi found that the supervisor was resentful and rude towards her, demanding ever faster production on the line. 'I really wanted to quit,' she says. 'I felt rotten. All week long it was the same thing. The only reason I didn't quit was because I didn't want to give him the satisfaction.'

Unfair practices are still going on at General de Cable. Last night, she says, the entire workforce was told to attend a union meeting. Conchi couldn't go, because she had a conflicting meeting at the daycare centre where she sends her two-year-old son. 'Now I will lose two days pay as punishment,' she sighs, with an air of resignation.

❊ ❊ ❊ ❊ ❊

With few exceptions, every twin plant has a doctor who visits the plant regularly and usually a nurse on full-time duty. However, many *maquiladora* workers claim that these measures are inadequate. In some cases the factory medical staff actually worsen the situation by not allowing workers to leave and seek proper medical attention in the government-run hospitals, or by incorrectly diagnosing and treating their problems.

Francisca González Rodríguez lives in a tiny house in the city of Nogales, Sonora, with her husband, a retired bricklayer, and 13 children, in-laws, and grandchildren. Francisca sewed luggage in a *maquiladora* belonging to the Denver-based Samsonite luggage company for eight years, and two years after quitting, still bears the scars. 'It all started when I'd been at Samsonite for about four years and they gave us this new material to work with,' she begins. 'After about eight months, I started getting a bad rash on my arms and legs. It was very itchy and it stung.'

Francisca went to see the plant doctor, claiming she had an allergy to the new material. She had never had any problems with the old material. The doctor told her it was impossible and declared the virulent red spots to be chicken pox. After applying a cream to her skin for forty days, the problem only got worse. Then the doctor told Francisca that she had a fungus and gave her a new cream, with the same results. Finally, with her legs by now bleeding, the doctor gave Francisca a devasting piece of news. 'You have leprosy,' she announced. Yet in spite of Francisca supposedly having such a serious contagious disease, she was never excused from work.

At least thirty other women working at Samsonite had the same painful skin condition, says Francisca. 'I still get angry about it because I don't feel I was properly looked after.' Recently she went to see a friend at Samsonite, who happens to be the sister of a supervisor. 'She got exactly the same condition as I did,' she says, 'but was immediately given time off. That's what I don't like. Maybe those creams might even have worked if I could have stayed off work. I went to personnel, I quarrelled, I asked for time off, not just for me but the other women who had the problem, but no.' Eventually, says Francisca, she was moved to a new production line and the problem, if not the scars, began to clear up.

Francisca believes nothing can be done about such problems in Nogales. 'You know why?' she asks, 'because here they only have to see that people are beginning to organise and they fire them all. At Samsonite, they fired 17 people in one go, just because they were defending their rights, some of them had worked there for 15 years .'

❊ ❊ ❊ ❊ ❊

Marta Alicia Oceguera has lived all her life in Tijuana, and worked in a half-dozen or so of that city's *maquiladoras* since the age of 16. Now at 23, an outspoken young woman with curly brown hair and a thin, fine-featured face, she has finally left the assembly line. Most jobs in Tijuana pay better than the *maquiladoras*, but Marta Alicia has found one of the few that do not. Having finished her highschool education by studying on Saturdays, she is now employed as a literacy teacher for US$33 a week by the National Institute of Adult Education (INEA).

Marta, who is divorced and looks after her five-year-old daughter Lilián, doesn't mind the change or the drop in wages. The job at INEA, she says, gives her a great deal of personal satisfaction. She sees little prospect for a decent life in the *maquilas*. 'I wouldn't say that's possible, because in the *maquilas*,' she says, 'it's just pure exploitation, you just can't rise above it. According to them, when you start, if you work hard, you'll move up and make more money, but they're just empty promises. They don't raise your pay, or give you better jobs to do, or anything. It's nothing but *puras vueltas*, pure evasions, and work, work, work.'

Marta now lives in an unpainted, two-room plywood shack with small windows and a dirt floor in a *colonia* called Mariano Matamoros. A sink for washing sits outside the house, and a few emaciated plants are anchored in the dry sandy earth. Because of the poor soil, rainstorms flood the place, she says. It's a two-hour trip to work on the chaotic transport system of privately-run buses and vans.

Marta's history in the industrial parks is a litany of poor working conditions and thin pay packets. Her last job was at a company called Vinil Tec de México, which belongs to Vinil Technology Inc, of El Monte, California, making cosmetic cases and plastic notebooks. She left two months ago, even though she was earning US$67 a week, almost double what she gets at INEA. 'The work there was really dirty and dangerous,' says Marta vehemently. 'We were working all the time with high powered machines, presses that practically strip the skin off your fingers, they're so hot, red hot. In the summer we were roasting inside the plant. There were no fans, only two ventilators to cool the machines, not for us. I had to buy my own aprons because my clothes got so dirty, and the company would never give us any.' The company also denied the workers masks, gloves or other protective gear. But they insisted on high production standards. Marta had to rivet the metal snap rings onto plastic binders as they came hot out of the presses, and was one of the fastest workers in the plant, yet she got into frequent arguments with the supervisors because of the poor quality of the materials. 'The binders would come out all bubbled and wrinkled,' she says, 'and quality control would send about two thirds of them back. Every supervisor had a different explanation, but it was always our fault. I told them, "it's one thing to be fast, and another when the material is no good."

I'd start slowing down, cleaning the press all the time, and I still got material rejected by quality control.'

Before working at Vinil Tec, Marta worked the night shift at another plant, called Levimex de Baja California, S.A., owned by the New York-based Leviton Manufacturing Company. They make circuit breakers and connectors or plugs for electric light switches. Marta's job was to wind fine metal wire onto bobbins. 'One night', she recalls, 'the machine went crazy on me, twisting the wire all up, and a piece of wire went into my eye. They took me to the nurse, who could hardly see the tiny piece of cable, and she put some drops in my eyes and that was all. But my eye was swelling up worse and worse - I wanted to go to the hospital, but they wouldn't let me.' With the piece of wire scratching her eyelid, and the pain steadily increasing, Marta finally persuaded the nurse to remove it with a pair of tweezers. They bandaged the eye, gave Marta a short rest, then sent her back to work. 'And you know where they sent me,' she says indignantly, 'to solder with a soldering iron, even faster work and with one eye. So I said, "look, this work is really bothering me with the gas from the soldering iron. You can't do this with one eye." And they said, "well it's the only job there is right now."'

Marta finally talked the supervisors into letting her go home, but the bobbin machine continued to give her problems and sent pieces of wire into her eyes twice more. The supervisor told her that she must be doing it on purpose because she didn't like working on the machine. 'And I said to him, 'Look, you think I would get wire in my eye for the fun of it?' In the end,' she says, 'they switched me to final assembly, but there I had to solder again, and the gases continued to bother my eyes. I went to see a doctor and he said to me, "you have two choices, keep on working there or keep your eyesight".'

Now Marta doesn't know if she'll be able to make a living as a teacher or have to go back to the *maquiladoras* some day.

❄ ❄ ❄ ❄ ❄

Fernando Godínez and Martina Alvarez, both in their late 20s, live together with Martina's 13-year-old daughter, Blanca, in a *colonia* in Ciudad Acuña called Aeropuerto. The family's home is more a collection of rooms than a house. One cement block room contains the fridge, a television set and a large bed. A narrow path separates it from the kitchen, a wooden frame covered with opened cardboard boxes, nailed firmly in place with bottle caps beneath the nails for extra grip. Inside there is a stove, racks of dishes and a small table. Beneath the ceiling a plastic sheet sags with water that has leaked through from the previous night's rain. In front of the cement room is another cardboard room where Blanca sleeps and behind the kitchen a fourth room, this one with a few pieces of wooden siding and an ancient red door.

Fernando and Martina make an odd couple. He has shoulder-length dark hair and was planning to go to the University of Chapingo near Mexico City when he came up to Ciudad Acuña to visit relatives, got a job, and ended up staying. Martina never made it through primary school and taught herself to read with an old bible. 'I guess I'm just stupid because I never learned to read at school, and I still can't write,' she says, although she agrees that learning to read by herself is probably a feat of some distinction.

Martina, like many working-class Mexican women, has a hard exterior, a tough skin of nonchalance until you get to know her. She has worked in various *maquilas* in Ciudad Acuña but dislikes them intensely. Last Monday she started at a Korean-owned *maquiladora* called Kim Toys, where the employees sew small cheap stuffed animals to go inside the ironclaw machines in the American chain of Pizza Huts across the border. 'It's the worst place I've ever worked in,' she says, while making supper. 'Rundown and dirty. And no air conditioning, just a couple of old fans in the whole place. It was so hot. Everybody just sat there sweating so much it looked as if someone had come in and thrown a bucket of water over them. I saw one supervisor get mad at a woman for taking too long in the bathroom. "Five minutes," he was saying. "All you've got is five minutes." She went back to her sewing machine and was crying.' Martina decided it wasn't worth US$30 a week and quit after just one day.

Fernando works at a plant called Arneses Y Asesorios de México, making electrical wiring for Ford cars, where he earns US$39 a week, plus about US$13 bonus for good attendance. Along with four others, the plant belongs to a company called Pep Industries of Nashville, Tennessee. Fernando has been there for six months, having moved there from a coupon sorting company called Indiana Data Processing de Acuña, where he worked for about two years. Before that, he worked for a company called Viniles de Acuña, which made vinyl beach mats and sports gloves for a company called Fibrionic II.

According to Fernando, the air inside the Viniles plant was terrible, filled with toxins emitted by the hot vinyl. He was among a group of workers who organised the factory staff to strike for masks and proper air conditioning. 'People used to get sick a lot and faint as well,' he recalls. 'And if you did get sick or injured at work, they wouldn't let you go to the IMSS because they didn't want their insurance rates going up. You had to go to a private clinic and pay for it yourself.'

The plant finally installed extractors, but for helping to organise the strike, Fernando and several other workers were fired. Fernando eventually won a settlement through the Labour Arbitration Board and used the money to buy the materials for the cinder block room. Viniles exploded and burned down in the summer of 1992, fortunately on a Saturday when no-one was at work. Fernando has heard that the workers are now operating in another plant, while crews are still cleaning up the mess of the wrecked factory in the Friendship Industrial Park on the city outskirts.

Fernando seems to accept his lot but Martina is fed up with being poor. Fernando has an uncle living in San Antonio, Texas who runs a small metalwork shop, and the possibility of going there has become more and more enticing to her. 'I can't stand this *colonia*, the poverty, the *maquiladoras*,' she says. 'They're all the same. Your life never changes. Sometimes I just get so desperate I don't know what to do.'

Fernando calculates that if he can scrape together about US$500 he can cross the border with Martina and look for a job in San Antonio. He realises that he'll still be poor there also, earning the US minimum wage, 'but at least it would be somewhere different,' says Martina. 'At least you could live in a clean, normal house.'

A lot of Mexicans feel as Martina does. In spite of the Border Patrol harassment, of being an 'illegal alien', of not speaking the language, things have got to be better for them in the US than in a dirty shanty town in Mexico. Every year thousands of them, from all over the country, take the risk and head for what they call 'the other side'.

So far, the couple have hung on in Ciudad Acuña. Fernando works in the plant and takes home his paycheque, while Martina dreams about leaving the jumble of rooms and going somewhere else, somewhere with four brick walls, proper floors, ceilings and windows. Somewhere in the US.

6

The Mexican Incident Book

Migrant Workers in the US

It was still light at six in the evening, but dusk was gathering in the shadows of the thick oak trees beneath which two Latino men were quietly chatting. The first of October 1992, the weather had yet to turn cold. The previous night, Leobardo Zarco from Mexico City, and Oscar Mendoza, a Guatemalan, had been sleeping rough in the ravine, along with a large group of other migrant workers. At that moment the rest of them had gone up to a nearby store to buy food. Because they had no money, Zarco and Mendoza stayed behind.

Suddenly they heard the sound of people crashing towards them through the brush. Five angry men wielding baseball bats appeared. Swearing in English, they demanded to know if the two men had had anything to do with a rape they claimed had occurred in the ravine the previous week. Also in English, both Latino men denied any involvement, but their reply made no difference. With a barrage of blows and kicks, the men came at them so suddenly that Zarco and Mendoza could not even attempt to protect themselves or run away. Within a few seconds, says Zarco, he lost consciousness. He doesn't remember being airlifted to a San Diego hospital where he woke up the next day in such severe pain that even heavy medication couldn't get him back to sleep.

By the time the five men ran off, Zarco had a smashed knee, internal injuries and a fractured skull. Mendoza had a broken right arm, gashes to the head and numerous cuts and bruises. Running out of the ravine, one of the five attacked 39-year-old José Luis López, who was standing by his car watching what was going on. López was left with severe cuts to his head and broken facial bones. Later, he had to go to a doctor in Mexicali for a series of operations that he had to pay off in monthly instalments, since he had no American medical insurance.

With its dried-up creek bed and plentiful brush and trees, the seemingly peaceful ravine where the attack occurred slices through a town called Alpine, an unremarkable community of 11,000 a few miles east of San

Diego. Groups of men numbering anywhere from 20 to 60 began spending their nights in the ravine about five years ago, the majority of them from Mexicali about 100 miles away. They share the place with lizards and gophers, and have accumulated a fair amount of garbage, strewing the stamped earth with wrappers, plastic bags and tin cans. At dawn, the men shake themselves awake, head over to the Circle K general store for a cup of coffee, then line up at the curb of Tavern Road above the ravine, waiting for contractors or local householders to come by and offer them work. They mostly get yard cleaning or painting jobs, aiming to keep their wages up at about US$4.50 or US$5 an hour and maybe get a meal thrown in as well. By the time of the incident, they were attracting contractors from all over the eastern part of San Diego County.

Although they worked cheap and provided the nearby grocery and general stores with continual business, the people of Alpine didn't like the men. Most thought of them as foreign, dirty and rowdy, invaders in their quiet, typically American town. They didn't like the garbage they left in the ravine or the way the men looked at the women. One resident complained to the press that women who attended his church had complained of 'lewd and lascivious looks', from the Mexicans. Scott Stewart, who published a small weekly called the *Jamul Shopper*, went so far as to write that because of the migrants, 'our women and children are no longer safe on the streets.' Another man, Raymond Ohm, publisher of a monthly called the *Mountain Empire Express*, said to the press after the beating incident, 'I refer to the whole thing as an infestation and to them as vermin. I look out my window and see them urinating against the trees. These men have no respect at all.'

One shop owner was so suspicious of his new customers that he began to keep what he labelled a 'Mexican Incident Book'. Ned Holmes manages the grocery store in the Alpine Creek Mall, just across the road from the ravine. Mostly, he and his employees noted down examples of shoplifting, half of which, during the cold months between December and March, consisted of socks. Another time he noticed the blankets used to cover produce at night had gone missing, and found them in the ravine the following morning. He also jotted down occasional drunken behaviour by migrants in the parking lot outside the store, and an entry about a man who stole beer contained the following, 'P.S. Some white boy beat the shit out of the Mexican down on Tavern Road.' Holmes admits that most of the migrants 'are just working people', who come over to buy tortillas, tins of refried beans, and barbecued chicken. Nonetheless, months before the incident he was prompted to write in the Mexican Incident Book that 'the way things are going, we're being forced to carry a gun'.

Others have kinder words. The owner of the mall's Earth Dancer bookshop says she feels ashamed to see the migrants subjected to such bad treatment. 'They're forced to stand there like cattle just waiting for someone to come by and offer them a job,' she says. Some of them, she adds, also make efforts to clean up the garbage in the ravine. Most of the problems, she believes, come from a few younger men who drink a lot after work.

Many migrants themselves concede that while the majority sit around talking and sharing a few beers or cans of pop, a few young men, often from the poor districts of Tijuana, drink heavily and sell or take drugs in the camp. In 1991, one migrant was killed by two younger men over an argument about paying for drugs. Yet no-one in Alpine sees any link between the brutality of the conditions in which the migrants live, far from family and never knowing if the next day will bring work or hunger, and the need for escape through drink and drugs.

Over the year before the beating incident, some of the townspeople got together for meetings about the 'migrant problem', but failed to agree on a solution. Some felt that a hiring hall or some kind of housing pavilion should be built, but far more residents countered that not only would this be a waste of their money, it would attract even more migrants to Alpine. As Sheriff's lieutenant, Sylvester Washington, puts it, 'We could never get anything resolved because the residents of Alpine aren't willing to spend one red penny on any kind of housing.'

Instead, various Alpine residents tried to think of ways simply to get rid of the migrants. One, George Vanek, an Alpine man who happened to be a San Diego County Grand Jury member, had tried for years to do just that. In 1991, he persuaded the rest of the Grand Jury - a temporary body appointed to listen to and decide if there is sufficient evidence for indictment - to compile a report on the situation. Released the following year, the document linked the migrants as a group to theft, drug use, and murder, as well as criticising their 'declining moral restraint'. It recommended that police sweep the camp regularly to hand out trespassing citations, in order to harass the men into moving away permanently. It also proposed that the ravine, which belongs to an Alpine lawyer named Bill Logan, be fenced off.

Local authorities, however, replied that the crime rate in Alpine had not risen since the migrant workers arrived. They found the report's recommendations to be unrealistic and unenforceable. Sheriff's Lt Washington, the Alpine substation chief, curtly explained that his two deputies had enough work already with a 103-square-mile area to cover. 'A person would have to be cited for trespassing three times before he could be booked into the County Jail', he pointed out, 'where he would then be immediately released.' Furthermore, because Logan's land was designated open green space by the county, special permission would be needed to fence it off. Other residents tried to get the Border Patrol involved, but at least 90 per cent of the men had green cards that allowed them to live and work legally in the US.

Many of the migrants in the Alpine camp have spent years working in various parts of the US. Zarco, for example, arrived in 1976 and found his first job as a waiter in a Beverly Hills restaurant. Some have homes in the state or just across the border in Mexico. Often used to big, fairly sophisticated cities like Mexicali or Tijuana, they know small-town prejudice when they see it. Many complain of being continually watched in Holmes' store when shopping just because they are Latino, and of people throwing rocks at them while they try to sleep. One man, 60-year-old Joel Rodríguez from Veracruz, reckons that Alpine is the most racist town he's ever known. The only reason he and others like him put up with the place is to find work.

Since the recession hit California hard, destroying an estimated 560,000 jobs since 1987, more and more migrants are turning to such precarious employment as they wait for the job situation to improve. The men are generally more assertive than undocumented workers and know their rights in the US. They realise that police officers are not allowed to ask them for identification without just cause. In the summer of 1991, when Alpine residents put up a sign by the road saying 'Curbside Hiring Encourages Homelessness. Please Don't!,' some of the workers contacted immigrant advocacy groups, who successfully petitioned the county to have the sign removed.

In late September, in a situation where racism was becoming respectable and blaming the victim the norm, the last spark needed was thrown into the powder keg. One Thursday night, September 24 a local woman claimed that she had been raped by three Latino men near the ravine. The following night her husband angrily went down into the ravine with a baseball bat and threatened the Mexicans there, but left without carrying out his threats. The police started investigating the rape charge. One week later, Zarco, Mendoza, and López were randomly picked out and attacked without warning. Suddenly Alpine and its now rather squalid ravine was in the public eye.

Zarco and Mendoza had been living in the US for 17 and 14 years respectively. Mendoza stayed with relatives in the San Diego suburb of National City, while Zarco shared a rented apartment in Pomona. Zarco had spent the last three years at a US$4.25-an-hour job in a chicken processing plant. He had decided to quit, he says, and earn money from casual jobs in Alpine, persuading Mendoza to come with him because he had heard there was lots of work. They had already lined up jobs for the following Saturday.

López, who lives in Colonia Ricardo Mazón Guerrero in Mexicali, also has his legal papers and had been working for a year as a mechanics assistant in a motorcycle repair shop in nearby Santee. He had a car, but used to sleep rough on a piece of cardboard in the Alpine ravine during the week.

At weekends he travelled home to Mexicali to spend time with his family and hand over his wages to his wife, Alicia, then pregnant with the couple's third child.

After the incident, some of the men began sleeping with piles of rocks at hand in case they were attacked again. Many left Alpine, seeking work in the lettuce, cauliflower and celery fields of nearby Calexico.

One man who stayed, identifying himself only as Alfonso, 32, has been living in the ravine for three years. Before that he lived in Tucson, Arizona, but the work there dried up. Every three or four months he crosses back into Mexico for the 24-hour bus ride home to Sonora state. The money he earns gardening and doing odd jobs never allows him to save enough even to share an apartment, he says, or to send much home to his mother. 'Things are very expensive here,' he remarks. 'After counting things like drinking water, sodas, and food, you don't have much left.' He washes in the mornings at a public tap and sleeps on cardboard and blankets at night. The men hang their few possessions in bags from tree branches - and during the entire time he has been there, no-one has ever tried to rob him. 'But yeah, it's hard,' he agrees, gazing around the ravine with its flattened grass and litter of dead leaves and rubbish. 'Sometimes it seems like all you have left is your hope - that still isn't gone.' Alfonso stresses that he is not illegal; he acquired legal residence status in the US eight years ago.

A couple of weeks after the incident, which did little to arouse the sympathies of Alpine residents, immigrant rights and Chicano activists in San Diego called a press conference. They condemned the attack in Alpine as indicative of the kind of racism Mexican workers had to deal with all over the US. Said Raymond Uzeta, director of the Chicano Federation, 'We wonder whether the self-appointed vigilantes would have made the attack if the alleged perpetrator [of the rape] had been Anglo. I think not.' All of the organisations present wanted the attack classified as a hate crime, a charge which would add four years onto any jail sentence.

For Immigrant Rights advocate Roberto Martínez, 54, who on behalf of the American Friends Service Committee (AFSC) has been documenting civilian, police and Border Patrol attacks on Mexicans for more than ten years, the Alpine incident was just another example of how Latin immigrants are scapegoated for all kinds of social problems. He attended town meetings in Alpine for a year, he adds, before finally giving up because no one seemed to want to do anything to help the ravine migrants. Although the District Attorney's office treated the attack on the three men as a hate crime, Martínez points out that previous assaults against migrants, including a recent one where Mexican farmworkers were attacked by Anglo men wielding steel pipes, have been dismissed by police as not racially motivated, because they were not accompanied by racial epithets. The AFSC offered a US$3,000 reward for information about the assailants of the three Latino men, which was quickly countered the next day by an anti-immigrant group, the California Coalition for Immigration Reform, who offered the same amount of money for information about the rape.

In fact, the rape proved difficult to investigate. 'We tried to put the puzzle together and make the pieces fit,' says Sheriff's Lt Washington. 'But they weren't there. They absolutely weren't there.' Police and even the FBI found themselves frustrated as both suspects and witnesses cited by the alleged victim told them that the woman had been drinking beer with some of the men and had often had consensual sex with them. The District Attorney's office was unable to prosecute because the accounts, as they put it, were 'vague and contradictory'.

On 15 October, the San Diego County sheriff's department arrested two men for the attack, 26-year-old Ronald Aishman and 22-year-old Ronald Inman. Shortly afterwards, three more including Dan Stout, husband of the alleged rape victim, were picked up by police and also charged with battery, assault with a deadly weapon and conspiracy. With the exception of Stout, none of the men was from Alpine itself and all of them had criminal records for incidents such as drunk driving and theft. One man, 28-year-old Charles Nocita, was even on parole. Stout had been arrested on a number of previous occasions - for wife battering.

❄   ❄   ❄   ❄   ❄

The incident in Alpine illustrates the broader issues confronting Mexican immigrants in the US. There now exists a dispersed community of millions of Mexicans on 'the other side'. Some with papers, others without, some travelling the endless circle back and forth from Mexico, others putting down roots within American society, Mexicans work at a huge variety of jobs, most of them low-paid. Much like the Afro-American community, Latinos often serve as a convenient scapegoat for all that seems wrong with American society.

Mexicans working in the US, both legally and without documents, are now estimated to number between five and seven million. The phenomenon is so widespread that remittances sent home to families in Mexico now constitute the country's fourth largest source of income. According to the Banco de México, workers' remittances fell 6.3 per cent in 1991, but in spite of the poor state of the US economy, recovered in 1992 to total more than US$2 billion, an 11.5 per cent increase.

Although it has been studied by many scholars and writers, it is difficult to quantify this migratory wave. In some cases the migrants are poor and see the US as the one place where they can make a decent living and earn money to send to those they've left at home. Others come out of curiosity or for social reasons, continuing a family practice that may have gone on for generations. Others are comparatively well-off, and have the means to make the trip and pay a '*pollero*' or '*coyote*' the hundred to five hundred dollars necessary to get them across the border, where their skills and education may open new doors for them. However, Mexico's economic stagnation over the last decade has meant that more and more households there depend on money from abroad. Start chatting to a stranger anywhere in Mexico and they are likely to tell you that they have worked in the US at one time or another, or have relatives there.

Mexican immigrants brave all kinds of dangers to get across the border. Some have died in refrigerated trucks, in locked railcars or after getting lost in the desert. Many more have made the crossing, or several crossings, successfully. Mexicans travelling north to look for work often plug into an extensive network of friends, family or people from the same town or village already living there. This 'network of solidarity', as one Mexican described it, helps find them a place to live and some kind of job which doesn't require English. They can even acquire false papers to satisfy employers and avoid detection by the Immigration and Naturalization Service.

Many communities in Mexico, especially small rural towns and villages with few decent jobs, have a long-standing tradition of sending men to the US. In some cases people who have never even been to a state's capital city make the journey north, knowing that they will receive help from networks set up years before. Heads of household from these states frequently return to their homes for holidays or when they become unemployed.

Although migration from Mexico across the northern border had been going on for many years, the roots of the current exodus lie in the Bracero Program. Set up in 1942, when the US joined World War II and found itself with a sudden labour shortage, the programme allowed thousands of mostly rural Mexican men to enter the US to work as *braceros*, or farm workers. Hired to pick cotton and harvest fruit and vegetables, Mexican men could cross the border on a temporary basis, until the programme was cancelled in 1964. Even before the Bracero Program began, Mexicans, like immigrants from all over the world, were attracted to the US. In 1930, for example, it is estimated that over five per cent of Mexico's national population lived in the US. Once the Depression began, thousands of them were unceremoniously sent back.

During the Bracero Program, nine Mexican states provided the bulk of the migratory flow, Pacific coast states such as Jalisco, Guerrero, and Michoacán; central states such as Guanajuato, Zacatecas, and San Luis Potosí; and northern or border states such as Durango, Chihuahua, and Baja California. Studies show that as late as 1984 these areas still provided 70 per cent of migration, an indication of the importance of the family networks established by the *bracero* migrants.

There has also been significant migration from the state of Oaxaca, as many Oaxacans had previously migrated to Mexico's northern agribusiness states such as Sinaloa and Baja California. Once there, they found themselves tempted by better paying farm jobs over the border in California.

From the late 1970s, however, the migration trends began to change as more and more Mexicans began leaving from large urban centres such as Mexico City. At the same time, large numbers of women joined the migratory wave, reflecting the growth of Mexican participation in all kinds of US service and care industries which employ women. Entire families have also been joining relatives amnestied by the 1986 Immigration Reform and Control Act (IRCA).

In 1986, after turning down many similar bills, the US Congress finally voted to approve the IRCA, also known as the Simpson-Rodino Bill. The bill introduced some of the most sweeping changes in immigration law since 1952. It allowed immigrants who had lived continually without papers in the US since before 1982 to apply for amnesty and regularise their status. Subsequent bills also allowed farm workers who had held 90 days employment between 1985 and 1986 to legalise themselves. More than three million immigrants - an estimated 70 per cent of them Mexican - took up the offer.

In an attempt to control immigration, IRCA also called for stepped-up border enforcement, including increasing the number of Border Patrol agents by 50 per cent. For the first time, fines of US$250 to US$10,000 per person could be imposed on employers for hiring 'illegal aliens'.

Although the Simpson-Rodino bill was intended to stop the flow of migrants, it has so far had little success. Hard data on current migration levels is hard to find, but the US Border Patrol reports that its nationwide apprehensions have risen steadily in recent years. In 1989 it caught 891,147 deportable aliens, rising to 1,146,914 in 1992, and to over 1.2 million in 1993, although numbers have yet to hit the peak of over 1.6 million arrests in 1986. Although the Border Patrol apprehends people without legal status in the US from over 90 different countries, well over 95 per cent of those captured are Mexican.

While the numbers are high and rising, two factors must be taken into account. One is the increased number of officers, from 3,180 in 1987 to a current figure of 4,130. The second factor is that many apprehensions are of the same person, who when caught, tries to cross again shortly afterwards and may be caught again. It also includes many Mexican shoppers or visitors who are not looking for work. Nonetheless the Border Patrol itself calculates that for every person stopped and deported, at least one to two others get through.

Over the 1980s, the employment picture for Mexican immigrants in the US has also changed. While previously most Mexicans worked on farms, that number has fallen to an estimated 15 per cent. The vast majority now work in service industries which boomed throughout the 1980s, such as convalescent care, hotels, restaurants, and building maintenance. Mexican migrant workers can also be found in light industry, such as food processing, electronics and garment making, and in construction.

Many factors contribute to the huge demand for Mexican labour in the US. One has been the deskilling of much of the industrial process, where manufacturing has been broken down into small, uncomplicated steps. On the other hand, the loss of certain skills among American-born workers, such as masonry, iron work, or shoe manufacturing, has made Mexican labour indispensable to American businesses in this sector. Since the 1960s, almost the entire labour force in California shoe manufacturing has been made up of Mexican workers from León and Guadalajara, both shoe-making centres in Mexico.

With the restructuring of the American economy, subcontracting has become a key to survival for many firms needing to cut costs. Often, more highly paid, unionised jobs depend on lower-paid non-unionised work supplying the firm with cheaper components. In this sense, much like in Mexico's *maquiladora* industry, American jobs can depend on cheap Mexican labour.

Studies have shown that it is the very status of the workers as migrants, with homes and families back in Mexico, that makes them attractive to American employers and allows these firms to stay afloat. Far from their families, Mexicans will work extra hours and days when necessary, and go home and rest up or visit family when not needed. That makes them more flexible than American-born workers. The flexibility allows companies to lay off workers and cut costs when business is slack and thus increase their competitivity.

According to University of California professor Wayne Cornelius, 'Small, immigrant-dominated firms offer a number of advantages beyond lower labour costs. Firms in the most competitive consumer-goods sectors and those responding to highly volatile consumer preferences (e.g. electronic games, personal computers, clothing) must have very quick turnaround time on sub-assembly and prototype work to ensure that their product reaches the market before those of their competitors. The small firms with their flexible (not just cheap) immigrant workforces can produce new items virtually overnight. Needless to say, such firms cannot offer their employees much in the way of job security or steady income.'

Service industries, on the other hand, cashed in on the availability of cheaper labour with no added social security costs, as more and more Americans found they could afford domestics or care for the elderly.

Furthermore, unlike American workers, Mexicans add no social cost to the US economy. Their education and training take place and are paid for in Mexico, as is that of their children. When ill or upon retiring, they will go back to Mexico, releasing the US state from paying old-age pensions and other costs.

The question of whether Mexican migrants have depressed wages is a prickly one in the US, as is the entire controversy over whether they harm or benefit the US economy overall. Some charge that, by being willing to work too cheaply, they have depressed wage levels, at least in local markets. Studies show that in many cases, however, they are competing against other migrants or with newly legalised Mexicans.

According to Douglas Massie of the University of Chicago, most research on the phenomenon tends to show Mexican immigrant labour complementing that of the US-born workforce. Where competition does exist, says Massie, 'it is weak or insignificant'. In Massie's opinion, immigrant labour has actually allowed a number of industries not only to remain but to expand in the US. One example he cites is that of the Los Angeles garment industry which, he says, 'is basically there because of the presence of immigrants in the labour market.'

Michael Greenwood of the University of Colorado and Arizona State University's John McDowell have found that 'the more narrowly defined the industrial sector and/or region in question, the more likely are investigators to find negative consequences of immigrants on native workers and earlier immigrant groups.' They go on, however to remark that 'offsets to such negative consequences exist, but since they are often spread through the economy among other workers, employers, consumers and regions, these offsetting forces are difficult to identify and especially to quantify.'

For Saskia Sassen of Columbia University in New York, the seeming contradiction between the existence of both labour shortages and unemployment stems from various factors which, she writes, 'generate differentiation within the labor supply and in the demand for labour. Among those factors are the price of labour, the expectations of workers, the need for certain types of economies to secure cheap and docile workers and the technological transformation of the work process in the last ten years that has not only upgraded some jobs but downgraded many more jobs, making them unattractive to workers with middle-class aspirations.' Those downgraded jobs, featuring low pay, no benefits of any kind, and no job security, have increased in number, says Sassen, to the point where they currently account for half of all jobs in the US. It is not hard to understand why employers can fit immigrant or undocumented workers so easily into such jobs.

A 1990 research report written by Jorge Bustamante of the Northern Border College in Tijuana underlines what he labels the 'spurious association between undocumented immigration and unemployment'. Bustamante's study of the effects of the IRCA points out that when the debate over immigration began and the first bills were introduced to

Congress in 1982, unemployment in the US stood at 10.8 per cent. By the time the Act came into law in 1986, however, and illegal immigration - judging by the Border Patrol apprehension statistics - reached a peak, unemployment had actually fallen to 6.3 per cent.

It is also evident that there has been an overall trend not only in the US but in other first world nations to keep wages down in order to compete more effectively with newly industrialising nations. This phenomenon lies behind the growth of off-shore manufacturing, as US companies have relocated to take advantage of cheap labour in poor nations. But for companies which cannot afford to move, immigrants will often accept lower wages than locally-born workers. In the search for lower-priced labour, many companies have also moved within the US to areas of the country, such as the South and the Southwest, where wages tend to hover around the minimum and unions are almost non-existent. At the same time, US labour unions have rarely shown any interest in organising or pressing for the rights of Mexican workers, especially those without documents.

National economies are never static and unchanging, and the role of immigrant labour is becoming increasingly important in many major economic powers. In the European Union 12 million migrants, according to some estimates, reflect a similar pattern to that occurring in the US. Turkish workers produce cars in Germany, while Moroccan labourers produce them in France, just as Mexicans and Asians manufacture electronic goods, shoes and clothing in the US.

Yet as in countries such as Germany and Britain, the immigration issue has become a convenient political tool in the US for dividing society and for removing blame from a system where homelessness is growing, where unemployed men brandish cardboard signs offering to work in return for food and where the Savings and Loan disaster of the 1980s is still costing tax-payers billions of dollars.

The greatest flaw in the argument that migrants, as opposed to debt or defence spending, are hurting the economy shows up in the growing labour shortage in the US. One reason that the demand for Mexican immigrant labour is increasing is the shrinking of the white, American-born population. Studies show that in the 1980s, in spite of immigration, the American workforce increased by only 1.5 per cent. It is expected to show negative growth in the 1990s, according to the US Census Bureau. In the 1990s, predicts the Hudson Institute, only 15 per cent of those entering the workforce will be white, American-born males. In 1990 the latest US Immigration Act actually increased immigration for fear of labour shortages. Where there is a demand for legal, controlled immigration, there is, it seems, an inevitable corresponding movement of those without documents.Up to 60 per cent of Mexicans entering the US illegally come to live and work in California. According to the Mexican consular office in Los Angeles, the city of choice for most the immigrants, one in four residents of that city is now Mexican or of Mexican descent.

This group, however, also has the highest poverty rate in the city - 22.1 per cent of Latinos live below the poverty line, compared to 21.8 per cent of Afro-Americans, 18.3 per cent of Asians, and 7.1 per cent of whites, according to David Hayes-Bautista, director of the Centre for Latin Health Studies at the University of California at Los Angeles. According to the US Congress' Office of Technology Assessment, the wages of Mexican immigrants are 20 per cent lower than those of other recent immigrants to the US.

As in Alpine, large numbers of immigrant men can now be seen on Los Angeles street corners and in front of large gardening and hardware supply warehouses waiting for a day's work. Along with low-paying service jobs, many Mexican women find jobs doing piece work, sewing or assembling in their own homes, often for little more than US$100 a week. In rural areas the bulk of farmworkers, many of whom are paid by the box or bucket and do not even receive a minimum wage, are still Mexican.

For many Mexicans, although life in the US is often an improvement over poverty in their homeland, it also means subsisting at the bottom of the economic heap. Often they live in substandard housing that at times rivals the shanty towns of Latin America. In El Paso the Mexican *colonia* known as Chihuahuita is the poorest and most crowded in the city, a far cry from the city's middle-class suburbs with their swimming pools and green lawns. Along other parts of the Texan border with Mexico, migrants, most of them itinerant farmworkers, live in colonies of shacks or old mobile homes, often devoid of services. In Los Angeles, the Latino *colonias* are plagued with poor housing, unemployment, and gang violence.

❊   ❊   ❊   ❊   ❊

About an hour or so north of the border, near the town of Carlsbad, Argimiro Morales, a Mixtec Indian from Oaxaca, drives out early one Sunday morning to talk to migrants at a typical camp of day labourers and farmworkers. Turning off the Carlsbad highway, he passes a vegetable farm where a few people are cutting bunches of green lettuce in the golden morning light and draws his truck up beside a steep hill, next to a row of bulging rubbish bags and a few ancient cars.

After crossing a narrow creek, the tall grass and weeds on the incline soon give way to woods. About halfway up, he comes to a small rubbish-strewn camp where five young men are making coffee. A blackened saucepan of water sits on the fire, a jar of Nescafé and a bag of sugar on the ground beside it. Under the spacious, shady trees, an ancient couch and a couple of old mattresses, piled with blankets and clothes, have been placed.

At the far end of the camp a makeshift shack with plastic roofing is precariously anchored to the branches of the trees. Beside it hangs a crude table, suspended by ropes. One man, rolled in blankets, still sleeps on the ground.

Farther up the hill stands the more established village, a sordid piece of third world poverty only a few miles away from the affluence of modern San Diego. About 500 people, mostly single men, live here in wooden shacks and lean-tos, their only source of water a tap at the farm. Some of the flimsy little structures in which they live contain no more than a mattress; in others, pictures are pinned to the plywood walls and old metal drums filled with burning wood serve as stoves. In one shack an old man cooks bacon and eggs in a huge skillet. The owners of the neighbouring shack have planted a small garden, surrounded by broken sticks affixed to black strips of plastic. Somewhere a radio is blaring, tuned in to a Mexican station.

The men at the camp know Morales from the Mixtec Popular Civic Committee or CCPM, an organisation he helped found in 1987. The CCPM works to safeguard Mixtec culture, and increasingly to provide much-needed social and legal services to Mexicans in California. He is warmly greeted by one man, a Mixtec farmworker named Salvador, sitting on a packing crate by an old table in the clear space among the shacks.

Salvador says he is 43 but looks much older. Married and the father of four teenage children, he has been travelling back and forth to the US for some 12 years. When he first arrived he says, he came with 'the idea to improve our lives, but I no longer believe that's possible.' The money he sends home has helped to improve the family house, but this year it is particularly hard to find work. 'The pay is really bad,' he adds - the most he can earn is a mere US$340 per month. But that is only 'when things go well and with a lot of sacrifice', he stresses. 'Sometimes you barely have enough to eat.'

Not all of the people in the community have legal residence permits. Salvador himself isn't sure if he would qualify for amnesty because he has come and gone so much over the years. In spite of his many crossings, he has never had a problem with the Border Patrol and never used a guide to get across. '*Ya sabemos el camino*', (we already know the way) he says knowingly. He owns a piece of land back in Oaxaca but because it isn't irrigated, it barely feeds his family. When asked about his future, he admits that he can only stick it out for another couple of months before once again heading home to Mexico.

Along the hill and down the slope stands the shack of one of the four families living in the camp. José and Catalina Mendoza have come up with their three children from the city of Cuernavaca in Morelos.

Her children just waking up, Cata is frying meat and heating tortillas over a metal drum with a fire going inside. Overhead, a length of plastic, dotted with dead leaves, has been stretched and attached to the various trees around the shack.

'José goes down every day and waits at the Country Store,' says Cata. 'Sometimes he gets work but sometimes he has to wait a long time. Almost always it's the weekends when he works because that's when Americans are resting.'

In Cuernavaca José was a bricklayer, but when he heard stories about how much money he could earn in the US, he scraped together the money to head north and try his luck. Over the years he has done various jobs around the city of San Diego, including one at a ranch which paid him only US$240 a month, until, he says, 'some friends told me about the Country Store, that you could get work there, just to watch out for the *migra*.'

According to José, the jobs offered at the Country Store usually pay US$5 an hour, but he adds, 'a lot of people only want to pay two-fifty. A few accept it - usually they're from El Salvador and Guatemala. They're there at the corner and they're getting US$20 a day with no meal, while I'm still there waiting. Someone comes by and says "you want to work?" and I say "sure", and he says, "well I pay US$3 an hour, over there on the corner they'll take US$3 an hour", and I say, "well you go ask them because I won't". I don't know why they work for so little,' adds José about the Central Americans. 'A lot of them even have special papers to live here. If I had a permit, even a false one, I wouldn't be there at all, I'd go look for a good job in construction, work for a big company.'

For the last five years, says José, he and Cata left their children living in Tijuana, going back and forth to visit them as often as possible. A few months ago, however, the three joined them in the camp. With pieces of scrap wood and other materials, José has built a series of three small shacks as well as a lean-to entirely covered inside with old brown carpet. Next on his list, he says, is a bathroom. The place bears a remarkable resemblance to the house of Fernando and Martina in Ciudad Acuña.

But without papers, unable to speak English, the Mendozas feel trapped. 'It's confusing,' admits José. 'Right now my wife and I don't really know whether to go back or stay. It's like everyone who comes from Mexico; down there they tell you that you'll earn a lot of money, buy a new car. It's not true.'

❋   ❋   ❋   ❋   ❋

While the depth of poverty in the Carlsbad camp seems incredible in probably the wealthiest state in the wealthiest country in the world, such living arrangements are commonplace among Mexican migrants. The AFSC's Roberto Martínez has found it difficult to convince authorities to improve the housing conditions of farm and day labourers. He recounts how during a series of meetings he attended to try and get a housing project for Mexican farmworkers in the area, locals came out against the idea. 'They would say things like, "we worked all our lives to get where we are, and why should these Mexicans just come up and get it all for free?"' he recalls.

The nightmare image of swarms of Mexican 'aliens' illegally crossing into their country and somehow taking advantage of them remains far more powerful for Americans than any amount of evidence that, if anything, the opposite is true. Their very illegality is what makes them so useful. What better way to keep a labour force docile, undemanding, and above all unorganised, than placing them under constant threat of deportation? Just as the people of Alpine missed the point that Mexican migrants would not be camping in their town if people were not continually offering them work, American society continues to fear migrants while hiring them to trim their hedges and lawns, and buying the products they help make more cheaply.

While the media, in articles on migration or the Free Trade Agreement, suggest that all that is lacking is the right kind of law and the right kind of law enforcement, their theories continually run up against the brick wall of reality. The two main factors that drive undocumented Mexicans to cross the border remain the demand for their labour in the US and the lack of opportunities and decent salaries in Mexico. There is absolutely no indication that NAFTA, like IRCA or the *maquiladora* programme before it, will make a dent in the flow. While US jobs pay better and there is an established network of contacts waiting there, a piece of paper bearing the signatures of three national leaders will mean nothing. If the Mexican economy and employment picture improve as a result of NAFTA, most students of Mexican migration predict that illegal immigration will actually increase, as more Mexicans will have the cash for a bus ticket to Tijuana or Matamoros.

Furthermore, the recent amendment to the Mexican constitution making *ejidos* private property - and thus saleable - will encourage millions of peasants to sell their plots of land and move to either large urban centres in Mexico or to the US. While NAFTA holds back agricultural imports from the US and Canada for 15 years after implementation, there is a growing belief that maize farmers, by far the majority in Mexico, will be drowned out in a sea of far cheaper grains in just a few years, once import barriers finally come down.

Meanwhile, the backlash against migrants in the US grows ever more vociferous. Organisations with a gloss of respectability, such as 'Light Up the Border' or FAIR - Federation for American Immigration Reform - as well as various English-only groups which campaign against even the most minimal services and education in Spanish, all operate on the assumption that Mexican migration is bad for American society and should be stopped.

Some of the board members of FAIR are former commissioners of the Border Patrol, an agency which has done a great deal to promulgate the image of illegal Mexicans as criminals through repeated violence against them.

These organisations received a boost when the Alpine case went to court in March 1992 and San Diego Judge Robert May removed the hate crime charge. May concluded that the men had acted using their freedom of expression, protected by the First Amendment of the Constitution. The city's Chicano and Immigrants Rights groups countered that this amendment may permit people to think what they want about Mexicans but does not allow them to act upon their beliefs with a baseball bat.

To the right of even these groups are various white supremacist and nazi organisations. Many of their members like to 'help out' the Border Patrol by hunting illegal aliens along the border at night. One such group sent a letter to Roberto Martínez saying 'Hello Beaners! Starting a war with the white man, down on Dairy Mart road? We will definitely accommodate you! We don't want any more greaseballs coming here illegally .... Your filth has been degenerating this country for years, and now the white man is going to act determinedly to stop you in your tracks.' It was signed, 'WARBOYS - A White Aryan Faction from the Great Aryan Nation.'

Such groups get their inspiration directly from the country's national and local leaders. San Diego mayoral candidate, Peter Navarro, has links with Light Up the Border and campaigned in 1992 with a platform calling for stronger measures to stop migration. Current San Diego mayor, Barbara Boxer, a Democrat, has since joined the anti-immigrant backlash, demanding that the National Guard be sent to help the Border Patrol swamp the border.

Back in 1984, then-CIA director William Colby mixed his racism with Cold War rhetoric and declared that Mexican migration could become a more serious threat to the US than the Soviet Union. Less than two years later, the 1986 President's Economic Report showed that illegal migrants produced more benefits than costs to the American economy.

During the 1992 presidential election campaign, Patrick Buchanan, a contender for the Republican ticket, came out against immigrants for causing not only violent crime but higher taxes, (this in a nation which earmarked US$239 billion for defence spending in 1994). 'What happened to make America so vulgar and coarse, so uncivil and angry?,' he asked. 'Is it a coincidence that racial and ethnic conflicts pervade our media when the racial and ethnic character of the US has changed more in four decades than in the past twenty?'

Also in 1992, California state senator, William Craven, chairman of the Senate Special Committee on Border Issues, said, 'It seems rather strange that we go out of our way to take care of the rights of these individuals who are perhaps on the lower scale of our humanity, for one reason or another.'

Craven, a Republican from the San Diego district of Oceanside, as well as other politicians, was having a political field day thanks to a report California governor, Pete Wilson, another Republican and close friend of Ronald Reagan, had released in late 1992. The report, put together by the state's finance department, was called 'California's Growing Taxpayer Squeeze', and blamed immigrants for placing an undue burden on government health, education and welfare programmes. Immigrants were costing the state so much money, claimed the report, that middle-class taxpayers were moving away.

In San Diego county another recent report calculated that illegal immigrants were costing local government US$146 million a year. But academics and immigrant rights activists called both reports flawed and biased. The numbers of illegal immigrants, they said, were inflated. By law, not even immigrants legalised by IRCA have the right to apply for welfare. The vast majority of both legal and illegal immigrants have no medical insurance at all, and must pay for health care. Those close to the border routinely go to Mexico for health care, because it is cheaper.

Furthermore, the costs Wilson referred to in his report included not only estimates for undocumented workers, but also for legal resident immigrants in the US and legally recognised refugees. Neither study took into account the billions of tax dollars paid by Mexicans living in the US and those who come over to shop, nor the very real economic benefits their labour has brought to the economy as a whole.

In 1993, Wilson stepped up his anti-immigrant campaign, calling for militarised border enforcement, an identity card for all immigrants in California, cutting services to immigrants and denying their children born in the US the right to US citizenship. Wilson has also attempted to persuade the Mexican government to monitor and reduce travel by Mexicans to the northern border. Wilson's actions, accused members of the Hispanic Bar Association at their 18th annual convention in San Francisco, had far more to do with promoting open racism and getting re-elected than trying to staunch the flow.

In early 1994, President Bill Clinton's Attorney General, Janet Reno, outlined a new plan to try to end the influx of illegal immigrants from Mexico. The US$367 million initiative will provide more than a thousand more Border Patrol agents and erect new solid steel fencing in the San Diego and El Paso areas.

Whatever the source, this attitude has made life for many Mexican migrants in the US precarious and filled with anxiety. In San Diego, two young factory workers, Armando, 30, from Guadalajara and Juan, 27, from Mexico City live in relative comfort compared to the hill camps. Both men share a 3-bedroom apartment with six other adults and three children in a nicely landscaped, grey-painted complex of apartments with wooden steps and railed walkways. Both men work for US$5 an hour in a San Diego factory that makes electronic pagers.

In five years as an illegal, Armando has never stopped worrying about being caught and deported back to Guadalajara. 'One lives with the incertainty, with the fear, that one day they'll catch you,' he explains. 'That's your daily bread. In truth, I've never got used to it; I'm afraid of it in the morning, in the afternoon, and at night. I think it's unfair because we've only come up to work, not to hurt the country.'

❆   ❆   ❆   ❆   ❆

The accusation that it is people like him who have brought unprecedented crime to the US is one that perplexes - and disgusts - Argimiro Morales. 'It makes no sense,' he says, 'how certain politicians in this city accuse us of being the sources of the high incidence of violence in this country. Why do they say this when in fact we are so often the victims? Drug addiction and gangs and violence are the results of this society, we didn't bring them.'

It is a warm weekday afternoon and Miro, as everyone calls him, has just come to the CCPM's small rented office from his job at a food processing plant in Vista, north of San Diego. In the larger room next door, the colourful remnants of a recent party held to celebrate the feast of San Miguel, patron saint of the home of many CCPM members, are still hanging from the ceiling and along the walls. Yellowed newspaper clippings and a poster of the ancient Zapotec ruins of Monte Alban cover one wall; next to them is a hand-lettered sign in Spanish quoting Lenin.

For Mexico's indigenous immigrants, some of whom arrive in the US unable to speak Spanish, let alone English, the fast-paced consumer society that confronts them conflicts with everything they have left behind. Some come from large Mexican cities where their parents migrated in the 1950s and 1960s looking for work. Others come directly from tiny villages where the land is still worked by hand, where roads are dusty tracks and water must be carried to the small stone houses by hand. Marginalised by their Spanish conquerors for centuries, victims of racism in their own country, they leave communities where families have known each other and followed centuries-old customs for generations, to live in crowded apartments overlooking free-ways and shopping malls filled with liquor stores and video arcades and gangs. Says Miro, 'the consumerism, the vices, conflict with our ways of seeing the world. They definitely conflict.'

One of the customs of the Mixtecs, who come from Oaxaca and parts of Puebla and Guerrero, is that of the *tequio*, a specified amount of time that is owed to the community in voluntary work each year. 'Whether this committee exists or not,' he explains, 'our people will come together and think about the problems in our communities. It is a tradition, a concept of life which the Mixtecs have, and which, in our communities of origin, is sacred. Here,' he adds, 'we cannot give the *tequio* in a physical way, so we do it by raising money.' Recently the Mixtec Committee sent money back to San Miguel Tlacotepec to install a drinking water system, saving villagers the more than half mile walk to the nearest river for water.

Their experience as workers in both the large ranches of northern Mexico and the factories and farms of California, has politicised the members of the Mixtec Committee. Along with an article about Nobel Peace Prize-winner Rigoberta Menchú, for example, one of their small monthly bulletins describes the May 1992 riots in Los Angeles, expressing solidarity with the Afro-American community there and suggesting that they had every reason to take to the streets. They also have been trying to forge a common front with other regional groups of Mexican immigrants in California. In Mexico, says Miro, their committee would be immediately stamped out. 'In our villages,' he explains, 'there are *caciques* who exercise such strong political control that our people are completely tied to the politics of the government. It is like a straitjacket. We would never be permitted to organise ourselves there the way we have here.'

The Mexican government likes to send its state governors on trips to California to visit migrants and look for votes, but when the governor of Oaxaca arrived, he got short shrift from the Mixtecs. 'Even the people in the hill camps told him not to come and see them,' recalls Miro.

A short, rotund man with curly hair, Miro first came to the US in 1982, working at all kinds of trades for years until finally getting his present steady job. Seven years after he left them behind in Oaxaca, his wife Teresa and their four children came to California to join him. Now his two youngest are among the best students in their school.

According to Miro, it used to be common for Oaxacan farmworkers to dig out small caves in the hills to spend the night after working in the fields all day. 'We have all had that experience,' he says, shaking his head and smiling ironically. 'You see, that is where the ranches are, the plantations of tomatoes and other vegetables, everything they sow here. So it never bothered the boss that there were people living in the bush or underground to hide themselves from the '*migra*' . The '*migra*' would arrive at a camp, but people were hiding underground, that's where they slept and everything. The boss never cared in what conditions the field workers lived. They worked all day and that was all he cared about. It's as if the idea of disposable paper plates is being applied to human beings.'

Since the 1986 amnesty, however, the sight of Mixtec and other indigenous field workers sleeping in caves has largely disappeared. Yet a host of other problems remain, including exploitation, racism, and outright violence.

'The bosses are voracious here,' says Miro. 'They say there are laws that they have to pay us well, but that's not true. We have had many cases in court against bosses that won't pay, that treat their employees badly. We had one where a rancher didn't pay ninety workers for three months' work. The government intervened and sent some of them back, but the Mixtec community helped them to get the money owed them.'

Miro also describes some recent examples of racism, including that of a group of youths who go out on the streets and fire paint bullets at Mexicans. 'Last month some boys shot real bullets at a man standing on the street waiting for someone to offer him work. They hit him six times and right now his life hangs by a thread. I don't know how he even survived.'

The Committee was originally formed to allow Mixtecs a place to meet and preserve their culture, but the group became both public and militant after an incident in Carlsbad in January 1990 involving a young Mixtec from Puebla named Cándido Galloso. The owner of a local store and his brother, tired of Mexicans standing in front of their business waiting for jobs, beat up Galloso, tied him with heavy tape, handcuffed him to their porch, and put a paper bag over his head saying '*No mas aqui.*' Various customers and even a Border Patrol agent saw the hapless Galloso during the three hours he was tied up but did nothing. Later a local police officer was quoted in the press as saying, 'They [the store owners] were frustrated pure and simple, but I don't think there were any racist overtones. ... A businessman loses thousands of dollars a year to shoplifters, people scaring away his good customers.'

That incident, which was not the first time the store owners had attacked Mexicans, drove the Committee to call a press conference and stage a protest demonstration in San Diego. The case even had repercussions in Mexico as the government there protested against Galloso's treatment.

But, says Miro, 'Our people still flee from the police, from other people, from many things. All they want is to work and save money, then go home. Sometimes from fear or whatever, if anything happens they don't even come to us to talk about it. Our problems exist in the shadows.'

✻ ✻ ✻ ✻ ✻

The Alpine attack case has been delayed in going to trial, because the decision over whether to consider it a hate crime has gone as far as the California Supreme Court.

A few months after the beating incident, the ravine in Alpine was finally fenced off. Men still gather at the curbside for work, while local residents take turns videotaping them and hand over the tapes to the Border Patrol.

Leobardo Zarco spent about a month in hospital, then was offered a place to live by a retired San Diego businessman named Bill Richardson, who had worked for many years with Central American refugees. For a long time, Zarco was extremely bitter about the whole incident. When an FBI investigator asked him one day, 'and what were you doing when the others went to the store? Eating tortillas or *carne asada*?', Zarco felt insulted by the ethnic barb and refused to talk to the press, or investigators or even to testify in court.

Eventually he moved to Tijuana, where he runs a food stall in one of the busiest, most rundown parts of the city only blocks away from the border fence. Surrounded by the cheap, degenerate hotels favoured by poor, would-be migrants, he now sells hot meals to men and women waiting to cross the border and look for work in the the country he has just left. 'The first few days after I was out of hospital,' he says, 'I didn't feel the same as before, I didn't feel as secure. Before, I was never afraid of anything, but now it's not the same. I don't know if it's like a trauma or what, but I feel more secure back in Mexico.'

He is calmer now, says Zarco, and ready to testify in the trial of his five attackers. He still limps a lot and the cold weather and rain bothers him considerably. Three times he describes the intense pain he felt after the beating, the many injuries to his battered body. The beating also made him realise how far away he is from his family. 'You miss having someone you can talk to about your problems, that's for sure,' he says, 'someone to call the doctor for you, to give you some moral support.' Nonetheless, he admits that once he is better, he will be heading back to the US to look for a job again. 'That's the only reason I came up here,' he says, 'to work.'

Oscar Mendoza had a steel rod put in his arm, which later broke and was left untended for months because he could not afford medical care. Unable to work, he had to leave his home and live in a shelter for the homeless in downtown San Diego. When the shelter closed down for lack of funds, Mr Richardson found him a temporary place to live where he could get work picking avocados.

Miro believes that working in the US can never resolve the problems of the Mixtec or any other Mexicans. Poverty, exploitation, and lack of democracy exist on both sides of the border. 'Working in the US is the first thing at hand,' he says, 'the alternative for now. But our future is still uncertain, too uncertain.'

7

Let's Shoot Some Aliens

The US Border Patrol

Margarita Tello de Miranda turned on the news on Radio XENY in Nogales one Saturday afternoon in June 1992 and heard that she had become a widow at 22. Her husband, Rubén Darío Miranda Valenzuela, 26, had been found dead that morning in Mariposa Canyon, just across the border in the US. He had been shot in the back twice.

Months later, sitting on a rumpled double bed in her mother-in-law's house, Margarita is still dressed in black. Framed by long curly hair, her large pale face is heavily powdered. The youngest of her two children, called Rubén Darío after his father, is running a battered toy truck across the uneven cement floor.

Margarita starts nervously and looks up at the ceiling at every question, every returning memory, then calms herself and answers in a thick northern accent. She gives the impression of wanting to say a great deal but lacking the education to explain herself on such a painful subject. When asked how she will look after herself and her two small children, she cries and does not answer. Luz Castro de Miranda, her mother-in-law, pulls a thin cotton housecoat modestly around her and runs her fingers through her hair, trying to look tidy, and, replying for her, says, 'Well, as best she can.'

Miranda had made the journey from Nogales to Tucson without mishap several times in recent years. He'd work a few weeks with his cousins, mostly on building sites, then head home again to his job in a workshop that repaired car upholstery.

According to Margarita, her husband had returned from Tucson only two months earlier, but by June work was scarce in Nogales once again. This time he took along a friend, Manuel Morán, and his brother-in-law, Eduardo Torres. Just before 7 o'clock in the evening, when the sun was about to set, they crossed over the three-strand barbed wire fence, which is all that separates the US from Mexico at that point, and walked about a quarter mile into a shallow brush-covered arroyo known as Mariposa Canyon.

Their progress was followed by five agents of the US Border Patrol. The spot where the three men had crossed, the closest to Miranda's home in Colonia Esperanza, was known as a busy corridor for narcotics shipments. They called it area 6-50. The agents had shown up there in the hopes of catching such a shipment and later said they were convinced that the three men were drug scouts.

Two of the agents, Thomas Watson and Michael Elmer, split off and took separate routes towards the men in an effort to apprehend them. Watson lent Elmer his personal semi-automatic weapon, an AR-15 carbine, which he was hoping Elmer might buy from him.

Upon approaching the trio, Watson shot several rounds into the air, then radioed Elmer that one of the now-scurrying men was heading towards him. He then heard further shots and headed to the area where Elmer was waiting. By the time he got there, he found Elmer, excited and elated, standing over the body of Miranda.

According to court reports, Watson told Elmer that they should report the shooting as an accident. But Elmer replied, 'No, I can't do that because I shot him six, eight times and most of them are in the back.' Instead Elmer wanted to drag the body over the border line and bury it in Mexico the next day.

Elmer also told Watson that he had seen something shiny and thought the dead man had been carrying a gun. When they examined the body, the shiny object proved to be a metal water canteen attached to Miranda's belt. Watson found Elmer's behaviour odd and went to look around the site for some evidence of a weapon or drugs, returning a few minutes later having found nothing. By then, Elmer had dragged Miranda's body down the slope to a gully and left it behind a tree. Pointing the AR-15 at him, he told Watson, 'We're never going to talk about this again once we leave this hill.' At some point in the next five minutes to half an hour, Rubén Darío Miranda Valenzuela died.

The pair rejoined the three other agents and returned to the station, where not a single detail of the incident was reported. Instead, they sat in the parking lot and drank a few beers. But Watson began to feel guilty. He couldn't forget the body left lying in the ravine. He thought about it all night and told his wife to take their children and leave town for a few days. In his pre-trial deposition, Watson stated, 'I was scared that Elmer would try to get rid of the only witness to the shooting - me.' At about noon the following day, he asked to speak to his chief, Joseph Marrufo, and told him what had happened. Then he went out with Santa Cruz County sheriffs and located the body of Miranda still lying by the tree in the gully.

Morán and Torres, running from the shots, escaped back into Mexico and went home. When Miranda didn't show up, they assumed that he too had managed to get away, and probably even completed the journey to

Tucson. That's what they told Marguerita at home with the children, who figured Darío would call that night. That afternoon, however, the first reports came out over the radio. Violence on the border is common, but the shooting death of a young Mexican - and the arrest of a Border Patrol agent - made the news.

❊   ❊   ❊   ❊   ❊

Margarita Tello met Darío Miranda when she was 15, at a party in the *colonia* where both had grown up. If she had never noticed him before, it may have been because he spent every spare minute playing soccer, a game for which he had a true passion. 'I fell for him all of a sudden, right away,' she recalls. Three years later, they were married, and less than a year after that their first child was born. For a few years the family lived in a crude three-room house of unfinished cinderblock, which Miranda had built near the crest of a steep hill in Colonia Esperanza. According to Margarita, the house was so cold during winter months that their daughter, Jasmín, was frequently ill. They decided to move in with her parents in a comfortable, white stucco house with a black-painted wrought iron gate, while Darío's parents moved into their old place.

Miranda never made much money for the family, and as Luz describes his various jobs it is easy to see why. One of nine children, his father a bricklayer, Darío always worked, even as a teenager, everything from packing groceries for supermarket customers for tips to selling popsicles in the street. He also worked in the *maquiladoras* and in shops making tortillas.

'Building us a proper house, that was his main ambition,' says Margarita, 'it was all he planned for. So that's why he'd go up to work with his cousins in Tucson, doing roofing and construction and that. There he could make good money.' Every time the car upholstery jobs dried up, which was fairly often, he made plans to go to Tucson.

❊   ❊   ❊   ❊   ❊

Darío Miranda did finally complete his journey to Tucson - to the coroner's laboratory for an autopsy report. County Coroner Bruce Sparks found that Miranda could have lived for as long as 30 minutes after being shot, and might even have been saved had he received quick medical attention.

Charged with first degree murder, Agent Elmer seemed unworried, even though the Border Patrol released his name to the press, something the force almost never does, regardless of the complaint. In spite of the seriousness of the charge, he was relaxed and smiling at his bail hearing, and pleaded not guilty.

By then, his lawyer, Michael Piccarreta, had made sure that Miranda was no longer just an undocumented Mexican worker making yet another trip up to Tucson to earn a few extra dollars to fix up his house. Shortly after the shooting, a Nogales radio station received a fax, purportedly a copy of a letter from someone in Mexico who knew Miranda. 'Darío Miranda was a drug trafficker,' said the anonymous writer. 'One day he had to meet a bad end. Don't judge Mr Michael Elmer too hard ...'

Piccarreta claimed that he had received the letter, hand written in Spanish and unsigned, ten days after the shooting. He denied having faxed a copy to the radio station but the fax letterhead proved that it came from his office. The letter raised suspicions for other reasons as well. It was postmarked in Tucson, and the date was written American style. People were referred to by their maternal last names, rather than the paternal one which comes ahead, and it referred to 'la Border patrol', while Mexicans routinely call them the *migra* or *la patrulla fronteriza*.

Civil rights groups accused Piccarreta of using dirty tactics and 'sowing hatred', but the damage was done. From then on, Darío Miranda was referred to in the press as a 'suspected drug scout', and was widely considered, at least in Arizona, to be so.

Linking the dead man to drug trafficking was effective. The war on drugs is one of the US government's favourite ways to place blame for social problems on something over which they seem to have no control, which is a law enforcement issue, and a product of the Third World to boot. The Nogales border station, located in the middle of one of the main drug smuggling corridors, had been making some of the largest seizures in history over the past few years. Only four days after the shooting of Miranda, for example, officials seized a 410-pound load of cocaine. With an estimated 50 per cent of all cocaine, 20 per cent of the heroin, and most of the marijuana coming into the US from Mexico, the Arizona Border Patrol has been responsible for the vast majority of the total US$1.4 billion-worth of narcotics seized in 1992, well up from the US$1 billion-worth captured in 1991.

So steady is the flow in the area that at one spot smugglers created their own gate in the chain link border fence. When migrants also started to use it, the smugglers put a padlock on it.

Yet vast amounts continue to get across. In Tijuana in June 1993, police found a 'narcotunnel' leading beneath the border from a warehouse in the Mesa Otay Industrial Park to another warehouse in San Isidro. Two years earlier in the small town of Agua Prieta, Sonora, authorities found a similar tunnel, running from the games room of a wealthy home to a warehouse in Douglas, Arizona. Authorities have no idea what quantity of drugs passed through the tunnels, but the American owner of a pair of popular snack and fruit juice bars in Agua Prieta said that his business halved after the tunnel was discovered.

Across the border, an environmental group trying to close down the Phelps Dodge copper smelter conducted a study into the economic impact on the town of the possible closure and found that sales receipts went up and down not in accordance to strikes or layoffs at the plant but with the marijuana harvests and rumoured drug shipments. In the small town of Río Grande, Texas, a community with no obvious means of economic support other than farming and a smattering of tourism, illegal drug smuggling is so common - and open - that there are many new mansions in and around the town, complete with walled yards, satellite dishes, gazebos and swimming pools.

Yet the irony is that in an area where those involved in the drug business on either side of the border have a lot of money and spend it fast, Miranda did not even live in his own house. When people suggest that her husband either worked for or was a drug dealer himself, Marguerita simply replies, 'Anyone who thinks Darío was involved with drugs should come and look at the kind of place we were living in,' referring to the roughly built house at the far end of Colonia Esperanza.

Even more ironic was information from an Office of the Inspector General (OIG) investigation that came out shortly after Elmer's first trial appearance. The OIG is the government department which carries out internal investigations for the Immigration and Naturalization Service (INS). Elmer's ex-wife, Tina Marie James, then remarried and living in Fairbanks, Alaska, told investigators that sometime in October 1990 Elmer and another officer had arrived at their home with five beige packages wrapped in blue tape, which contained five kilos of cocaine from a recent drug bust. On 24 October, Border Patrol agents had seized 4,391 pounds of cocaine near Nogales, the largest-ever haul by border guards. Elmer had said, she claimed, that they could sell the narcotics for US$50,000. However, according to James, the couple used quite a bit of it at home themselves. When Elmer signed on to fight in the Gulf War in January 1991, James took up with a new man, who also helped himself to the drug. That same month an anonymous letter slipped under the door of an OIG official in Washington tipped the agency off to the drug theft, yet even after the investigation no charges against Elmer were forthcoming.

James had another piece of intriguing information for the OIG investigators. She recounted a conversation with Elmer several months after she had remarried, when he bragged about having stopped a group of marijuana smugglers and shot one of them in the knee, possibly shooting off the leg. The wounded man had then been dumped over the fence in Mexico. The man, 19-year-old Jesús Luna, had been promised US$250 that night in October 1991 to bring over a backpack filled with marijuana and leave it on US soil. After being shot and left bleeding on the ground in Mexico, he had to have his leg amputated and is currently suing the INS for US$4 million. Border Patrol spokesmen, however, say that Elmer was not on duty the night that incident occurred.

Over the past two years, however, the Arizona sectors of the Border Patrol have been plagued with corruption. In 1992, a head mechanic was indicted for defrauding the government, and the chief jailer put on probation for robbing prisoners. Douglas agent Ronald Backues was given a 12-year sentence in December for ferrying shipments of marijuana in his Border Patrol vehicle and a former agent, also based in Douglas, received a life sentence in February 1993 for trafficking in cocaine stolen from smugglers. Another Arizona agent, Willie García, went to prison in December for perjuring himself to defend an accused heroin smuggler with whom he maintained an intimate relationship.

❊ ❊ ❊ ❊ ❊

Months after the loss of her husband, Margarita admits that while life still goes on without him, she finds it hard to sleep at nights. She thinks about him and worries about how she can support two small children. She misses him waking up early in the morning to go running, and the neighbourhood kids coming by to see if he wants a game of soccer. 'All I feel is a great sense of loss, of pain,' she says, from the house where her mother-in-law still lives.

The house is the furthest up a difficult, rocky hill, muddy and barren. It is made of unplastered grey cinderblock, partly divided with an unfinished wooden wall. The back room is a dark, crowded kitchen with a few battered appliances and helter-skelter shelving. On an old wooden bureau against the wall, lies a flat cardboard box of candy which Luz sells on the street.

Across from the formica table, Luz is lying on her bed, chatting with her sister and an elderly friend, who are sprawled on pillows on the cement floor. When Margarita and Darío Jr walk in, they get up abruptly and silently leave, allowing the two women to talk about their lost son and husband.

For both women the idea that Darío met such a solitary and painful end out there in the desert is perhaps the most horrible aspect of the whole incident. 'I just think of him there alone, still alive, and animals biting him and things like that,' says Margarita. 'That's how I think of it.'

When asked what she is hoping for now from the courts, she answers, 'Well, we don't want him [Elmer] dead or anything, we're not bad like that. But he should pay for what he has done, because he has caused us a great deal of pain. The Border Patrol has done many bad things in the past, but this is the worst.' Luz mentions that while listening to a call-in show on the radio recently, she heard a Nogales waitress of Mexican heritage phone in and talk about Elmer. 'It seems that he and the other officers used to go the restaurant she worked in every day,' she recounts, 'but Elmer never wanted her to serve him, he wanted an Anglo waitress. He hated Mexicans.' If there is a war going on along the border, these two women, who at times still seem in a state of emotional shock, are its most obvious victims.

❆   ❆   ❆   ❆   ❆

The sun is setting, turning the PEMEX towers and the silver cupola atop the barrel-roofed cathedral in downtown Reynosa pale gold. Parked on a picturesque winding road lined with green grass and trees, the yellow brick chimney of an old water pumping station up ahead on the right, Pete Ibáñez is sitting at the wheel of his pale green Chevrolet Suburban, waiting for an 'illegal' to emerge from the willow brush. A radio controller has just alerted him that one of the sensors has been tripped.

'I used to work as a manager in a Sears store up in Corpus,' he explains, 'but it got so that I'd go in and spend the whole day behind closed doors, not even knowing whether it's raining out, or sunny. I began to ask myself what was I doing with my life, what would I tell my grandchildren. I looked around and decided that I wanted to do something to help my community. That's when,' he says, turning slightly, 'I decided to join law enforcement.'

Ibáñez is a tall man, still young, with pockmarked cheeks, a moustache and an easy-going, rather kindly air. Originally from San Antonio, he likes to chat as he patrols his sector of the border, keeping an eye out for aliens. 'I feel pretty good all right every time we get a drug bust,' he says. 'I say to myself, well, that's one shipment that won't end up in the neighbourhood or near my kids' school.'

A few hours earlier in Hidalgo, he and agent Juan López caught three people from Reynosa, a middle-aged woman and two teenagers - her son and a nephew. Smelling of sweat and river damp, they sat behind the metal grill in the back of the Suburban and told him that they were only crossing to do some shopping. Later, he picked up a young man after checking his ID at the town's other mall. Julio César said he was 20 but looked much younger, and claimed he too had only come across to buy something and was about to head back to Mexico. Ibáñez also watches for Central Americans, but now that the wars are pretty well over there, he has far fewer of them coming through. Central Americans are detained and if they don't qualify for political asylum, deported back to their country of origin, while Mexicans are immediately sent back. 'If you send back a Salvadorean or Guatemalan, thinking he's a Mexican, then he'll just try and come over again the next day,' says Ibáñez.

Passing again through Hidalgo, the small town right across the river from Reynosa and the first stopping point for illegal crossers, Ibáñez checks out

Cisnero's Restaurant in the Don José Plaza, a small shopping mall. Often, he explains, this is the first place people head to once they've made it across. Taking out his binoculars, he can see the signallers sitting on the international bridge. They make signs or use walkie-talkies to let the '*coyotes*' know when the '*migra*' is there, and again, when they leave and in which direction.

Most of the time, Ibáñez drives patiently along the narrow dirt roads by the river, over vine-covered irrigation ditches and through thickly growing brush. At least twice a day the dirt roads are dragged, leaving their surfaces smooth and finely dusted to detect footprints and tire tracks. Agents call it 'cutting for sign'. It seems a relaxing activity, worlds away from San Diego where most agents must sit in their vehicles, watching the crowds amassing at what they call the '*bordo*', the edge, waiting to charge across as soon as the coast is clear.

At one point Ibáñez stops and points out the faint ridges ribbing the grassy plain leading up from the river. A few years ago, he says, this used to be a field of melons. Now the Nature and Wildlife Department has been buying up strips of river bank and letting it go to brush. Quickly overgrown with weeds, willow, huisache trees and the small yellow flowers local people call girasol, or sunflower, they make perfect hiding places for drug smugglers or border crossers. In some spots, the agents find inflated rubber tubes hidden in the brush, used to ferry migrants back and forth across the river. 'We bust them up, whenever we find them,' he explains matter-of-factly.

A system of sensors, strung out along the winding river border, helps the Patrol find the border crossers. The majority of them are seismic, sending out a signal to a radio controller when they pick up vibrations from foot steps or a passing vehicle. Any large animal like a dog can also set them off, however, and crossers eventually get wise to their presence, noticing the spots where people are continually caught. Then the sensors are dug up and moved to another spot. Other types of detectors use infra-red radar or are magnetic, especially useful if a car or truck passes by.

Every time he catches an illegal border crosser, Ibáñez stops his vehicle and fills out voluntary repatriation forms for each of his detainees, interviewing them in Spanish. Then he drives them back to the bridge and sends them across the chainlink-fenced walkway back to Reynosa. He points out the rolls of barbed wire along the walkway nearest the customs station, put up to prevent people from climbing out. They still find shreds of clothing on the wire, showing that people are willing to risk cutting themselves for a quick return across 'the line'.

Ibáñez says that he's not into violence or danger. He takes his time and waits patiently if the radio controller reads out a number indicating that a sensor has gone off. 'It's not worth getting shot at or breaking a leg or something,' he says, 'just to capture an illegal or two.'

❉   ❉   ❉   ❉   ❉

The Border Patrol office in MacAllen, Texas, out of which Ibáñez works, is a flat, modern brick structure topped with an American flag, near the city's small Free Trade Zone by the airport. Inside, secretaries and controllers beaver away, while the agents, most of them Chicano here, write up their reports, question and detain illegals, look after their equipment, and send people back to Mexico. The posters on the wall are reminiscent of picture books or puzzles from the 1950s, green-uniformed officers with a little tow-haired boy, or a Collie dog, or his horse. They reflect a way of thinking that has never quite made it into the 1990s.

Border Patrol spokesman Mario García is a chubby, affable man who has been with the Patrol for 17 years. Slowly and carefully, like a school teacher, he explains the mechanics of his outfit's job. The farthest east of Texas' five sectors, MacAllen covers 20 counties including the border. The river meanders so much here that, although they watch over about 70 miles of it as the crow flies, the actual mileage of frontier is over double that figure. With 340 agents, both men and women, the MacAllen sector in 1992 ranked number three nationwide in arrests, after San Diego and El Paso, and number two in narcotics interdictions, after Tucson. 'Arizona has a land border,' explains García on the high numbers of narcotics arrests in that relatively unpopulated part of the country. 'It doesn't give smugglers any obstacle whatsoever. The Río Grande does give a buffer zone in there, which is why we're not number one in narcotics interdictions [even though] we've proven to be the newest corridor for narcotic influx into the US.'

As the enforcement branch of the American Immigration and Naturalization Service, the Border Patrol was formed in 1924 out of remnants of the disbanded Texas Rangers, mainly to catch tequila smugglers. Now it is responsible for patrolling areas between ports of entry, according to García. 'Therefore the main objective is to apprehend people, to act as a deterrent to people who are trying to get into the country, right? To do that we have units which are readily identified, aircraft, agents on foot, on horseback; we patrol the border in a very visible manner to try to pose a deterrent.'

With the passage of the IRCA in 1986, he adds, the Patrol was also given the job of checking businesses 'that were known, or where we had information, to be hiring illegal aliens.'

Besides stopping people at the border, the patrol also combs streets and public places for illegal aliens inside the country. 'We have the responsibility of checking all modes of transportation,' explains García, 'commercial airlines, buses, freight trains - those are checked on a daily basis at their point of departure.'

García refutes claims that the Patrol indiscriminately picks out people who look Mexican from crowds and demands their documents. 'I'm sure you've heard stories about that,' he says in his circumlocutory way, 'but please understand that the Border Patrol is a law enforcement agency and has always had the responsibility, legally with respect to being prepared to go and respond in court, say in a case about discrimination or whatever, to be able to articulate why he chose to question any particular individual as to his citizenship or right to be in the US.'

Yet even while agents are ostensibly trained for this kind of work, physical appearance still plays a great part in their decisions to stop someone. 'Obviously we know that over 90 per cent of the population here is Hispanic right?' says García. 'So what do we look for? We look for clothing, mannerisms, for speech. Speech because if you compare, just to give you an example, a Cuban or a Salvadorean or a Nicaraguan, or someone from the south or central region of Mexico, accents are obviously going to be different from the way people speak Spanish here. At one time,' he adds, 'when we were dealing with the typical *bracero* type, field labourers, [stopping people with particularly Indian features] might be true. Then you were more likely to run across a person wearing *huaraches*, a type of shoe that is not used on the border, you would look for a person that looked like he'd worked on the land his entire life. So those are some of the keys that we used.'

'All in all,' says García, 'I think you'll find that when you get away from the stories about reported abuse and what not, you'll find that the Border Patrol is a very professional organisation.'

Over the years, however, the Border Patrol has acquired a reputation for brutality, much like the Texas Rangers who preceded them. For a long time, border rights activists have been calling for more women and Hispanic agents, yet even though 41 per cent of the Patrol's officers are now Hispanic, the accusations of abuse have in no way dissipated.

Part of the problem stems from the accelerated war on drugs. Previously the Patrol was only authorised to go out and look for illegal aliens, not narcotics. If they found drugs, it was usually while looking for border crossers. Over the past ten years, however, that has changed, as the agency has taken on the task of looking for and seizing narcotics, and to do that, received increased equipment and firepower. With the agency now authorised to investigate reports of smuggling, without calling customs to handle the arrests, 'the Border Patrol,' says García, 'has been leaders in the interdiction effort.'

While their many narcotics interdictions have 'put [them] in the limelight', as García says, they have also undoubtedly jaundiced the view of many agents against migrants. As the supervisor of the Border Patrol in El Paso sector, Miguel Arras, laconically puts it, 'Well, where you find the aliens, you find the narcotics. The two of them run together.'

Frequently it is at the checkpoints on main arteries heading north from the border that both illegal migrants and drugs are detected by agents and their sniffer dogs. Here too, the agents may stop people at random and search their vehicles. 'Our agents there,' says García, 'are already looking for drugs in addition to aliens. Anyone coming to the checkpoint that might fit a specific profile, or some of the tendencies a human being might show when he is extremely apprehensive about something - you look for specific types of vehicles, odours, all kinds of things. I couldn't even begin to tell you all the things these agents look for.'

But García did give a few examples. Agents might stop a car, he said, 'that is so masked - because they've heard that a strong odour will trick the dog - with de-odoriser or perfume that it is noticeable, usually to hide the smell of marijuana. Or [similarly] the smell of new paint when the car has an old paint job, or a vicious dog beside the driver, a driver who doesn't particularly fit the description of what he is telling you he does or where he's going. So,' he concludes, 'you have an agent who has become so attuned to what to look for that they can readily turn around and tell you - "there's aliens, there's narcotics".'

As for illegal border crossers, according to García, agents have 'found illegals hiding under hoods of cars, hiding in car trunks, in hidden compartments, and in all kinds of vehicles from recreational vans to compact cars. Once we found two people lying on the dash board with all kinds of bags and quilts lying on top of them.'

The checkpoints, however, have come under repeated criticism, especially in the state of California. In the town of Temecula, near a checkpoint on Interstate 15, five people were killed in 1992 when a car chased by the Border Patrol crashed in front of a school. The Patrol admits that over the past few years, 24 people have been killed as a result of high-speed chases originating at their two San Diego checkpoints.

Unlike many agents, however, García is fairly sanguine about the huge number of Mexicans and other nationals they are unable to capture. 'Let me tell you, being the son of immigrants, I know the call of the US or the magnet of the US will never fade away,' he opines. 'It will always be the greener pasture to peoples all over the world. I don't think you'll ever have enough people to seal the border. I don't think our political structure would lend itself to an operation of that sort because our country's not based on that.'

But he sees no contradiction in keeping people probably quite like his immigrant parents out of the greener pastures. 'Being who I am, my responsibility to my job is the same,' he says. 'I've been in law enforcement for 24 years. I was a police officer before coming here, and I had to arrest Hispanics then. My job is my job. This is the career I chose.'

✳ ✳ ✳ ✳ ✳

Yet in spite of the air of restraint manifested by agents like Ibáñez and García, and although agents have been known to save Mexicans' lives, help deliver babies and let people go at times if they seem really hard-up, a woeful array of statistics presents an image of an enforcement branch that is continally abusive and dismissive of what they call the 'illegal alien'. In the past ten years, agents of the US Border Patrol, people like Ibáñez and García 'just doing their job' have:

- run over and killed Luis Eduardo Hernández, a 14-year-old Mexican boy who had just crossed the cement levee of the Tía Juana river into San Isidro in August 1989. Together with a group of some 100 people, Hernández and his brother were attempting to flee back into Mexico when he fell down the levee and into the path of the vehicle.

- shot dead 17-year-old Víctor Mandujano in the heart after chasing him and his brother back to the border fence in September 1990. The agent, who was in plain clothes, knocked the teenager down, hit him, drew his revolver, and shot Mandujano twice. The agent then pointed the gun threateningly at bystanders. The San Diego county coroner's office confirmed that there was evidence of 'muzzle stamp' on the wound's surface, meaning that Mandujano was shot point blank. The agent claimed that he was shooting in self-defence and that Mandujano tried to grab his gun thus shooting himself, a story denied by all the eye witnesses.

- shot dead Humberto Robles, a 33-year-old handicapped Mexican man, in the forehead on Dairy Mart Road in San Isidro in November 1990.

- shot dead Julio César Galicia, a 26-year-old presumed-alien smuggler in East Texas in November 1990.

- caused the drowning death of sheet-metal worker Armando Valenzuela by pulling and causing to capsize the inner tube raft on which he and three others were trying to flee back across the Río Grande to Ciudad Juárez in June 1987.

- shot and killed Rubén Navarrete Tarín on the levee of the Río Grande in El Paso, as he was trying to escape back across to Ciudad Juárez in May 1991. Border Patrol agents claimed that Navarrete was a drug dealer. They also shot 25-year-old Enrique Arguelles after he was allegedly seen bringing bags of marijuana across the river. Agents claimed both shootings were in self-defence and both were later acquitted by grand juries.

- killed 17-year-old Ismael Ramírez, in Madera, California, by throwing him violently against the pavement, causing skull fracture and brain haemorrhage in February 1988. Six years earlier, the same agent, Michael Lewis, struck and killed a Mexican man with his patrol vehicle in Calexico. In 1985 in Fresno, Lewis and other agents physically assaulted two undocumented farmworkers. A year later, Lewis was accused of beating a lawful permanent resident farmworker about the face even though the man was trying to show him his papers. The man was locked in the patrol vehicle, held for seven hours without charge or being allowed to call a lawyer and strip-searched while in custody.

- killed four Mexicans, including a seven-year-old girl, and left 16 injured, during two high speed chases near Laredo, Texas in the 1980s. The agent, Robert Handy, shot at the driver of a pickup truck carrying illegal immigrants triggering the crash in the first case. In the second, he crashed his vehicle into the back of a sedan, killing two illegal immigrants hiding in the car's trunk.

They have also shot and seriously wounded:

- 12-year-old Humberto Carrillo through a large hole in the chainlink border fence in Tijuana in April 1985, while the boy was allegedly raising a rock in one hand because an agent was beating up his older brother, still on US soil. Lawyers for Carrillo, who won US$574,000 in damages in 1992, noted that the rock story did not figure in the agent's account of events to internal investigators, and that Carrillo had been shot in the back.

- 15-year-old Eduardo Zamores, who earned money carrying shoppers' parcels for them, while he was straddling the boundary fence at Calexico/Mexicali in November 1990. The 9mm hollowpoint bullet severely damaged the boy's left lung, liver, stomach and intestine.

- Rosa Pineda, a 24-year-old Salvadorean woman and Francisco Carbajal, a 16-year-old Mexican, by shooting into the back of the van in which they were being smuggled with eight others on California Interstate 5 in May 1990.

- Francisco Ruiz, 22, in the stomach, when he tried to stop a border agent in San Isidro in May 1989 from abusing his seven-months-pregnant wife, Evelyn (she was later jailed for sixty days for 'misdemeanour illegal entry' and assault). Ruiz was charged with assaulting a federal officer but acquitted after implausible testimony from the agent who said that Ruiz had hit him with a rock, that his gun had fired by accident as he fell over, and that he had then suffered amnesia.

- 15-year-old Pedro García in the stomach, in El Paso in August 1989. Agents then held García down and told him he was going to die. Agents later claimed that García was brandishing a rock; García maintains he was gesticulating and yelling because agents were beating up his friend, Arturo Beltrán, 18. García was treated, charged with assaulting a federal officer, but released six days later; Beltrán was convicted of illegal entry and spent 90 days in prison.

❋   ❋   ❋   ❋   ❋

Such instances are only a sample of the evidence showing that many Border Patrol agents are, to say the least, trigger-happy. According to an Americas Watch Report of May 1992, 'Since 1980, Border Patrol agents have shot dozens of people along the...border, killing at least 11, and permanently disabling at least ten. In addition, the Border Crime Prevention Unit... was involved in 26 shootings in which 19 people were killed and 24 wounded.' Yet with the exception of Michael Elmer in Nogales, no Border Patrol agent has ever faced criminal charges for any of these actions, although plaintiffs have won money from the federal government in civil lawsuits. In some cases, agents accused of shootings have subsequently been promoted.

Beatings are also common. Both the AFSC's Roberto Martínez and the San Diego Public Defenders office keep albums of photographs of the victims.

A typical example occurred on 18 July 1989, when a woman in Stockton, California, heard noises outside her apartment. From her balcony she saw a Border Patrol agent kicking a Mexican man, who was handcuffed and lying on the ground. When the woman shouted to the agent to stop, he bellowed back at her, 'Mind your own fucking business, lady'. The agent continued to beat up the man while the woman watched.

The Americas Watch report contains eight other examples, including beating already-handcuffed Latino men in the kidneys, brutalising others with their flashlights and batons, and even using an electric shock apparatus. Youths are also frequently beaten. In 1990, an official of Mexico's Interior Secretariat announced that a high percentage of deported juveniles complained of beating, shoving, threats and verbal abuse by the Border Patrol. During one lawsuit initiated in 1982 after agents raided a California mushroom farm employing illegal immigrant workers, an officer admitted to lawyers that often illegals were referred to as 'tonks' by his colleagues. They were called that, he testified, because that was the sound the agents' flashlights made when hitting Mexicans on the head.

In El Paso, Texas, a Chicana woman legally residing in the US was charged with assaulting Border Patrol agent Mario Bellamy in June 1992. Evangelina Alcocer's mother and sister were visiting her from Mexico when agents entered her neighbourhood of Paisano Apartments, a low income public housing project. Agents locked Alcocer's relatives, including a toddler and an infant, in the back of their unmarked Ford Bronco truck and went to look for more illegals. Worried about the 103 degree heat, Alcocer opened the door of the van to allow her family members to wait outside. When the agents returned and saw what she was doing they began to hit her mother and her, even though she was holding her own one-year-old baby in her arms. Witnesses say they saw Agent Bellamy repeatedly kick and slap Alcocer, before she sprayed him with mace, and was promptly arrested.

She eventually received a US$100 fine. The Mexican Consulate in that city cites two other accusations against Bellamy, one from a fruit vendor who had his face smashed and nose broken when shoved against a Patrol vehicle, and one from a detained woman who was injured by his reckless driving.

Border Patrol agents in El Paso have also routinely violated the rights of students at Bowie Highschool, just near the border. Nineteen-year-old David Ramírez, an American citizen, had almost got used to agents stopping him, asking him for ID and checking his bag, until a lawyer from the Diocesan Legal Aid office conducted a lecture at the school on the students' rights. Shortly afterwards, Ramírez was once again stopped by the Border Patrol, but refused to do anything other than declare his citizenship. He was then pushed up against a chain link fence, hit several times and verbally abused by the enraged agents, one of whom said to him, 'What do you think? You're a fucking lawyer!' Ramírez, as well as other students, faculty and staff, brought a suit for civil rights violations against the Border Patrol in 1992 and won. District Court Judge Lucius Bunton issued an injunction, warning the Patrol to stay away from the school, concluding that 'No justification existed for the force used against numerous plaintiffs and witnesses.'

Over the years, there have also been several allegations of the rape of undocumented women by Border Patrol agents. The one that earned most attention involved Agent Luis Esteves, who sexually harassed and raped women on various occasions in El Centro, near Calexico, after stopping them and checking their immigration status. In one case, a teenager was picked up by Esteves, driven to a motel, and beaten, raped and sodomised for over four hours. The 17-year-old girl, who had forthcoming deportation proceedings when Esteves stopped her and checked her documents, told police that the agent offered to help her and requested her phone number, then suggested they meet for a date. In the autumn of 1992, Esteves was convicted of one of the rape charges and sentenced to 24 years in prison.

In 1989, the FBI began investigating the allegations of a young Mexican woman living in a migrant camp in a canyon near Encinitas, California, who claimed that she had been sexually assaulted the previous September. The woman, who worked cleaning houses in Encinitas, said that the agent had demanded to be taken to her home, insisted on searching her, then sexually assaulted her.

In another case in Van Nuys, California, in 1992, a Border Patrol agent was accused by six Mexican women of kidnap and rape. The agent was imprisoned for 22 months and put on trial, but the jurors found him not guilty of all counts except false imprisonment, and he was released for time served. Prosecutors and social service agencies protested against the verdict, saying that it would deter future victims from going to the authorities with complaints. 'It particularly sends a message to undocumented women that you are not going to be believed,' said Sandra Cavacas of the Los Angeles Commission on Assaults Against Women, 'that you're at the bottom of the totem pole.'

It has been difficult for any human rights body to gauge exactly how frequently captured undocumented migrants are abused by the Border Patrol. The agency itself says it only receives one complaint for every 17,000 people arrested. The Immigration and Law Enforcement Monitoring Project, an AFSC-sponsored organisation that functions all along the border, reports about 142 complaints every year compared to the Border Patrol's 26. In Calexico, California, the El Centro Asylum Project documented over a dozen cases just in 1990, where people testified that they were beaten by INS officers during detention. It is not far-fetched to suppose that large numbers of deportees, precisely because of their illegal status, are afraid or unable to register a complaint, or believe that there is no point in doing so. Accustomed to even worse violence and corruption at the hands of Mexican law enforcement agents, many migrants may not find the abuse meted out by the Border Patrol to be all that significant.

The Border Patrol also frequently carries out raids on workplaces suspected of employing undocumented Mexicans. According to Americas Watch, 'Raids often employ many agents to make relatively few arrests. But their symbolic value is clear: through an impressive show of force, they remind undocumented migrants that they are subject to arrest and deportation at any moment.'

According to Stephen Kean, public relations officer at the Border Patrol headquarters in San Isidro, the agency carries out random checks using a survey of companies in the southern part of the state. They also receive several tip-offs a week from anonymous callers, reporting 'aliens' in both homes and workplaces. Sometimes particularly unscrupulous employers who do not want to pay their illegal workers for a contract job call the Border Patrol themselves once the job is done, so that the employees will be deported without being paid.

Agents have been known to break into workplaces and homes, without identifying themselves, and to frisk and handcuff people without giving them a chance to prove their status. During raids on farms, at least 15 Mexican workers have drowned while trying to escape officers by crossing irrigation ditches. In El Paso, a lawyer working for the Diocesan Legal Aid service in that city found out by accident that the Patrol sometimes stopped municipal buses and carefully worked their way through all the passengers inside. When he called the bus company to ask about this illegal activity, the controller told him, 'Oh yeah, it happens all the time. Why, did someone complain?'

Detention conditions and treatment in INS facilities, some of them privately run, are often terrible. People convicted of no crime, merely awaiting hearings for permanent residence or refugee status can spend months and even years in fenced compounds. Inside, they are subject to the whims of the staff and can be punished for the most minor infractions or misunderstandings. In one case, two 16-year-olds being held in detention near Brownsville, Texas, charged an INS guard with sexually molesting them.

According to the law, children in custody in Texas can be held in detention until claimed by a parent or guardian. Adults who are not related or who cannot prove guardianship are not allowed to take the children away, even if they promise the judge that they will bring them to a set deportation hearing. For minors or orphans escaping conflict in Central America, finding a parent has been impossible. In a few cases, youngsters have escaped violence in their homelands only to find themselves locked up for years in the US.

Few Border Patrol agents have the *laissez-faire* philosophy displayed by Pete Ibáñez or Mario García in MacAllen. In San Diego's Imperial Beach sector, a statue donated by an admirer portrays a Border Patrol agent holding a net and a chicken by the neck. The chicken represents a *'pollo'*, the slang Mexican term for an illegal border crosser. San Diego is also where the first Hispanic INS Commissioner, Leonel Castillo, was referred to as 'Chief Tonk'.

'Racially discriminatory attitudes ... pervade the Border Patrol and often become flagrant as agents along the southern border attempt to enforce immigration laws against Hispanics,' says the Americas Watch report. 'These attitudes are shared by many local law enforcement officials and persons residing lawfully in cities and towns near the border, who xenophobically fear that an influx of Hispanic migrants will undermine their employment opportunities or have an otherwise negative impact on the quality of their lives.'

The prevailing attitude among agents is that illegal immigration is like a huge tidal wave threatening to drown everything that is great about America. 'Maybe some of them are just coming over to work,' says El Paso Border Patrol spokesman Doug Mosier, 'but they also commit all kinds of petty theft, crime is up, thefts are up, insurance premiums are sky-high now in El Paso. Sometimes I think they should just open the border and let people see what would happen, the chaos. Just open it for a month so people could see the results.' An agent in Nogales adds, 'This whole thing with these illegals coming over in droves is just disgusting. It's disgusting what they're doing to this country, the way they take advantage, and all those human rights groups defending it. You people up in Canada just wait because the same thing is going to happen to you.'

In September 1993, the Border Patrol in El Paso set up what it called

'Operation Blockade,' totally blocking the usual illegal entry routes by parking agents and vehicles within sight of each other. According to Mosier, daily apprehensions fell from a peak of 1,200 a day in August to around 50 by November. Business in the downtown shops fell drastically, as determined border crossers were forced to cross into neighbouring New Mexico and walk back to El Paso. Yet while the Border Patrol and local police claimed that crime fell between August and October, when the statistics were compared to October 1992, it emerged that crime rates had actually risen.

❊ ❊ ❊ ❊ ❊

Roberto Martínez has spent over ten years documenting abuses of Mexican immigrants along the border, as well as going to meetings, protest demonstrations, court hearings, and visiting migrant camps. He has a small office in downtown San Diego, the city where he was born and grew up. Yesterday he helped set up a press conference on the Alpine incident and comments on the good turn-out. 'When I got back to the office,' he remarks, 'I got a call saying, "those guys got what they deserved. We don't want them here in our city, we don't want them here in our country. They should all go back to Mexico and you should go with them".'

Martínez is a heavy-set, soft-spoken man who never seems to lose his sense of purpose and calm. A fifth-generation Mexican who grew up speaking English, he has been living in the middle of a race war almost all his life. As a child, he went out to the fields to work with his parents. While still in highschool, he got part-time jobs washing dishes and remembers the kitchens being raided by the Border Patrol and all the Mexican workers being hauled away. He was advised not to bother graduating because he could always get a job as a labourer.

Martínez didn't graduate, working in a factory instead, but started going to night school, where he eventually qualified as an engineer. He married and moved his family to the San Diego suburb of Santee, where someone broke into his house and carved anti-Mexican slogans on the walls, and someone else burned a cross on the lawn of the black family across the street.

Mexican-American children at the school his own children attended began getting harassed by the Youth Klan Corp and by the police. That's when Martínez started fighting back. He initiated lawsuits and built a reputation. People started phoning him, about one third of them American citizens, to tell him what had happened to them. In 1982, he got a job with the American Friends Service Committee documenting these cases.

Martínez's grandparents moved to California from Texas in 1915, he says, because of the lack of opportunities there and the racism that dogged their lives. Now 56, Martínez is himself regularly stopped by the Border

Patrol and asked for proof of citizenship. Now that they know who he is, they harass him at home as well.

For Martínez, the current state of affairs is essentially a continuation of the racism Mexicans have always suffered, ever since Mexico lost its northern half to the US in 1848. 'It's more than just a coincidence,' he points out, 'that the Border Patrol was formed the same year the Texas Rangers were dissolved.' The Texas Rangers terrorised Mexican villages along the border for years as well as conducting frequent raids into Mexico, supposedly chasing bandits but more often attacking innocent townspeople. 'It has taken a different form this generation,' says Martínez. 'In the 1930s they just rounded up Mexicans and sent them all back to Mexico. In the 50s they had Operation Wetback. Now it has a lot to do with the economy. People can blame Mexicans for their economic problems, accuse them of taking jobs away from Americans.'

Dismissed as a crank by the police, the Border Patrol and city politicians, Martínez continues to collect daily incidents of maltreatment and racism against Latinos. 'Just before you arrived,' he says one morning, 'I got a call from an Ecumenical Centre here in the city. It seems two Border Patrol officers were chasing two undocumented youths and one of them ran inside the Centre. Without a warrant or anything, an officer chased him inside and caught him. Then, the people there tell me, the guy started banging this kid's head against the wall saying, "see what happens when you try to run".'

'The climate is changing dramatically with the border and the emphasis on law enforcement,' he adds. 'We have communities in North County now where it's about education. People don't want second-generation Mexican kids going to school with their own kids, having to hire teachers who can speak Spanish.'

'I think,' he says, 'that history is going to record the 1980s and 1990s as the most violent time along the border. You've got so many different levels of violence, by local police, the Border Patrol, Customs and special SWAT teams, like the one that existed between 1984 and 1989. They killed 20 or more people along one 14-mile section of the border. They would confront undocumented poeple in plain clothes, without identifying themselves and so people would often think they were armed bandits. If they ever raised a hand or a fist to defend themselves, they would always be shot.' According to Martínez, nine youngsters between the ages of 12 and 17 were shot by the Border Crime Prevention Unit in San Diego before they were eventually disbanded. 'Many were shot in the back,' he adds, 'running back to Mexico.'

'Now we have vigilantes attacking people, raping women and shooting. We haven't really tied them down ideologically, but they are primarily white gangs operating down there by the border.'

Martínez cites one particularly shocking case which occurred in May 1990. A group of young men spent the day drinking and taking drugs in the house of a friend on Monument Road in San Isidro, near a popular spot for illegal crossings. 'Let's shoot some aliens,' Dwight Pannel, 24, suggested to his friends. Stepping out on the balcony, Pannel took aim and fired. His target was Emilio Jiménez, a 12-year-old Mexican boy. Together with his uncle, brother and sister, Emilio was trying to rejoin his parents in Orange County. The Jiménez parents hadn't seen their children in two years. Four days after his death, they were finally reunited with Emilio in the Orange County mortuary.

But Pannel, who had previously attacked two illegal immigrants with a baseball bat, pleaded guilty to involuntary manslaughter and received only two years in an honour camp, a minimum security institution, getting out early for good behaviour. His drinking buddy, Leonard Cuen, used a bow and arrow to rob undocumented migrants in March 1990, but was never prosecuted.

'There have also been cases of drive-by shootings in North County,' continues Martínez, 'or incidents where Anglos drive up in a truck and hit a Mexican on the head with a baseball bat, or steel pipes, or they run people off the road. I've got files of hate crimes going back ten years, but the authorities don't call them that because they say there were no racial slurs.'

Organisations like FAIR, says Martínez, give a veneer of acceptability to such crimes. 'There are a lot of fringe groups who get their information from FAIR,' he adds, 'the supposed costs of illegal migration and so on. They have a lot of former Customs and Border Patrol commissioners on their board now.'

Politicians running for election in 1992 also used immigration as a convenient scapegoat for all that is wrong with the US. Recently, says Martínez, the AFSC organised a counter-demonstration to a White Supremacist march at the border. A truck ran over their literature table. Inside the truck, on the passenger side, witnesses noticed a then-candidate for state senator named Joe Fields.

For Martínez, however, the events that most stand out for him are the shootings at the border, especially of youngsters. Yet he also points out that there are many people who phone his office saying they wished they could do something to help. 'You always get those too,' he adds, smiling pensively for a moment, as his answering machine takes a phone message from a woman named Ramona, who wants to know what she can do to help the migrants in Alpine.

❊ ❊ ❊ ❊ ❊

In late 1992, Martínez was honoured as an 'international human rights monitor' by Human Rights Watch, a global watchdog organisation. Yet as the Border Patrol remains unrepentant and unbowed, as more and more politicians and community leaders, even liberal ones, succumb to the arguments of the right and call for their reinforcement, he faces an uphill task.

In December, 1992, after a federal court trial in Tucson, Michael Elmer was found not guilty of murdering Rubén Darío Miranda Valenzuela by a jury of eleven Anglos and one Latino. The jury accepted the Gulf War veteran's contention that he feared for his life when confronted by the unarmed man. In March 1993, lawyers in Tucson filed a federal tort claim and civil rights complaint against Elmer on behalf of Miranda's family. In February, 1994, a federal court jury in Phoenix, Arizona, also found Elmer innocent of the charges against him.

Elmer resigned from the Border Patrol on 6 April 1993. Thomas Watson was fired about a week later - for not reporting the Mariposa Canyon incident until 15 hours after it happened.

8
On the Line
Organising for Change in Mexico and the US

On 1 January 1994, the day the North American Free Trade Agreement came into effect, an event occurred which catapulted Mexico and its social disparities into news headlines around the world.

It occurred not on the northern border, but at the other end of the country in Chiapas, near Mexico's southern border with Guatemala. A couple of thousand insurgent Indians organised, armed themselves and took over six towns and municipalities in a rural, impoverished state. They demanded an end to five centuries of racism and misery, and to the fraudulent and unjust system in which all Mexicans live. Their desires seemed both simple and at the same time impossible, expressing, and in turn fuelling, the sense of anger and exploitation that has always been there in Mexico, but which most preferred to ignore. Behind the clean new image of a modern Mexico that the PRI has been selling to the outside world, Chiapas exposed the raw flank of another Mexico free trade negotiators would rather not see.

Free trade between Mexico, the US and Canada is but one step in the plan for a hemispheric trade bloc. The strategy is not so much about trade, since most of Latin America already enjoys preferential trade status with the US, but about Latin American nations bringing their economic policies and practices into line with those of the US. By 'locking in' existing investment laws, international trading pacts are particularly advantageous for the foreign investors so desperately courted by all of Latin America.

For Canada and the US, trade is nonetheless an important aspect of NAFTA. The opening up of Latin America's vast market is an obvious boon for US exporters. Then there is the additional advantage of using the cheaper labour forces of those countries to carry out at least parts of the manufacturing process itself, as in the *maquiladoras*.

What this means for the working class of these nations is anything but favourable. They are faced with cuts in the most basic services, such as health and education, and must increasingly fuel the great machine with their labour power at ever lower rates of income in capital's race for competitiveness. Situations like those seen along the US-Mexican border, with its wide array of problems, will only increase and intensify.

While it has become fashionable for business writers, investment consultants and analysts to preach the cause of Mexico, the liberalisation of trade and investment has done nothing or very little for most Mexicans. As in Chiapas and elsewhere, this is brutally evident along the northern border. Mexico's cheerleaders ignore these people's fierce desire for change, and their capacity to bring it about through their own actions rather than waiting for the materialisation of presidential promises of prosperity for all.

In the spring of 1993 in the city of Tijuana, lashed that year by severe rainstorms and floods, the 570 workers of a factory that makes plastic hangers for a Boston-based company called Carlysle Plastics Inc got fed up; fed up with the low wages, the six-day working week, and a gruelling production schedule that had them assembling and boxing twice as many hangers per shift as their American counterparts. They were fed up with the constant heat and the smell and fumes of melting resins and plastics emitted from machines that were never switched off. They were fed up with the treatment they received from their bosses and supervisors, and with company rules that could suspend them without pay for reasons as trivial as showing up one minute late on the assembly lines, for wearing a dirty apron, for chatting or listening to music while at work, for running, getting into an argument, or telling jokes that, in the words of the statute of regulations, 'alter the order and discipline of the company'. Women workers were even obliged to tell management if they became pregnant. The food in the cafeteria was inedible and the bathrooms often had no toilet paper or running water. But most of all they were fed up because they had no means of complaining about these problems.

The Plásticos de Bajacal workers decided that they needed a union, but when they went to the Labour Secretariat to find out about registering it, they received an unpleasant surprise. They already had a union. It was called 'Modern Mexico', and affiliated to the CROM, or Regional Mexican Workers Confederation. 'It's a union that protects the bosses, not the workers', says one Plásticos activist, Miguel Ceja López, 26. Eventually the workers found out that the CROM had secretly signed collective contracts with *maquilas* all over the city, and that they even ran an office in Los Angeles where they could contact US businesses directly before they went down to Mexico to set up twin plants. The CROM is a lucrative business, earning a reported US$20,000 per contract, plus weekly union dues which are paid directly by the factory in order to keep its workforce in the dark.

Despite the barrage of paperwork and legal niceties, and even though 15 employees were fired for their attempts to form the independent union, they were eventually successful. Throughout the difficult process, they actively sought publicity and the support of both other *maquila* employees and US workers across the border. 'We're doing this in a very public way,' explains Miguel, 'to motivate other workers, give them an example that through struggle, we can win.'

One of the activists they contacted in San Diego was a burly young construction worker named Tony Hernández. 'Yeah, I gotta get down there', he says, trying to ignore the constantly ringing phone on the desk in his makeshift office in the abandoned Carpenters' Union Hall. The place is being used by several hundred striking drywallers until it is sold, and is crowded with young men chatting in Spanish or playing draughts using old bottle caps on pieces of cardboard. They are all either just back from or about to go out to pickets throughout the city. 'The thing is I got so much work here I've had trouble finding the time,' he adds.

Hernández is in the middle of another union movement, this one largely made up of Mexicans who are legal in the US and working in the building trade. Since June 1992, they have been on strike for higher wages, medical benefits and most crucially, an independent union. No existing union has ever approached these men, and all of the organising, which resulted in some 4,000 of them finally going out on strike throughout southern California, was done entirely at the grassroots.

Tony has worked as a drywaller - someone who heaves and nails into place the 100-pound slabs of paper-covered plaster walling inside the wooden frames of new houses - all of his adult life. After putting on the drywall, another worker, called a taper, sands and tapes over the cracks between the plaster board making a smooth surface. Whatever their trade, all of them have seen a steady erosion of their wages in recent years that many have dropped below the poverty line.

Tony was born in Mexicali, where his father was a first class bricklayer and tiler. When he was 14, the family moved to Sacramento, California, where they had relatives. Still a teenager, Tony began working as a builder's apprentice. After two years, he could join the union and was earning US$12.97 an hour. By 1979, he says, he was making almost US$20 an hour plus health benefits.

'Then [Ronald] Reagan took office and in '81, they more or less broke the air traffic controllers strike,' recalls Tony, 'and started replacing them, so the unions lost their strength, especially in the construction industry.' According to Tony, the industry started a so-called two-gate system, 'one gate for union workers, and one for non-union workers, and there were at least 80 per cent more people coming in the non-union gate. And that wasn't Hispanics,' he adds, 'that was Anglo guys.'

Still wages stayed high. 'That was the strategy of the developers and subcontractors to destroy the unions,' he points out. 'They were offering you higher wages, and in those days you could buy your own insurance for about US$200 a month for a family, so it was worth it because you were getting US$200 to US$300 more.'

In 1986, the year the Immigration Reform and Control Act was signed, large numbers of Mexicans came north to join newly legalised families. 'Most of the guys started teaching their families and brothers-in-law and so on, people from their own villages and towns, to do construction work,' says Tony. 'So there was a Mexican boom in the industry. The contractors started getting rid of their Anglo workers, because they were earning say 18 bucks an hour and they could hire somebody who didn't speak English and have a bilingual foreman. If you were working in the fields for US$4.25 an hour, [and they] offer US$7 or US$8, of course you're going to make the jump.'

'People from Mexico took those jobs out of necessity,' he adds. 'Say you're earning US$30 a week down there and you come up here and you're earning US$100. You live in an apartment with 15 other guys and send US$40 a week home. There was nobody who ever said to them, "Look, you hold out and you can get US$10 an hour instead of US$6, and we'll help you."'

In 1990, when the Hernández family moved to San Diego, Tony was shocked by the low wages and high cost of living. He tried getting a job in commercial construction but was fired when he complained about being paid less than the Anglo workers. He went back to residential construction, and a heavy fall in wages.

'This is piece-work rates,' he explains. 'It's up to you how much you want to earn. There's no hourly wage, just the job.' Subcontractors had become very popular with developers, who paid a lump sum to them to get the job done, and they in turn hired construction workers, offering them so much per square foot of work. With the current craze in much residential housing in southern California for cathedral ceilings and archways, it was no longer a question of throwing up the drywall on essentially box-like structures. As Tony puts it, 'you really had to hustle'. One weekend, he adds, there were so many curves to be cut and finished on the entrance of a new house that they took him and three other men a whole day to complete. At the end of the day, they worked out that they had made less than the minimum wage, only US$10 a day each.

Like drywallers all over the state, Tony found himself working 10 to 12-hour days as well as weekends. Yet at the end of each week, the amount of money he took home was paltry. All during California's housing construction boom, wages had been going down. 'But then came the recession,' says Tony, 'and they just dropped the prices without saying anything. We'd move from one project on to the next and the prices were always lower.' In 1991 prices dropped again and he realised that he was down to the minimum wage, earning the same as the field workers who had come into the industry in the mid-1980s.

In 1992 Tony learned that another drywaller, a man named Jesús Gómez, was organising workers in Orange County, just north of San Diego. He decided to join the movement. 'I had hurt my wrist and had been even working injured for a while,' he recalls, 'but then I got Workman's Compensation [injury benefits] and decided to work full-time as an organiser, first in Orange County, then in San Diego. Instead of going to work for 10 or 12 hours, I'd go out to the job sites.'

Tony logged about 15,000 miles in his car, combing building sites to talk to the builders there. 'I'd explain to them how, when I started working, you could buy a brand new truck for US$3,200 and you were earning US$16 an hour. Now you're getting US$4 or US$5, and the same truck costs US$20,000. It just made no sense. So we explained the advantages of being in a union, of being organised, and that if we all work together, we can do it.' Most of those he talked to were Latinos, from Mexico or even Guatemala and El Salvador. 'We talked to everybody,' he says, 'and I mean everybody. I talked to Anglo workers and they just called us union busters. They don't understand. They were the union busters. They said "it's for you to fix the problem" and I'd say, "we are trying to fix it but we need your help".'

Those initial meetings in Orange County attracted perhaps 30 or 40 people, Tony recalls. Then the numbers started to double. When he started organising in San Diego, he began by meeting people in public parks, then they managed to get the Carpenters' Union Hall one night a week.

'A lot of people came up and on 1 June 1992, we decided we'd better go for it,' says Tony. 'We already had Orange County, Los Angeles and San Diego. In three days, we had 800 men out, right here in San Diego.' They began by marching on the San Diego County administrative building to publicise the fact that public works projects were being given to subcontractors pocketing a portion of the state-stipulated US$12.49 an hour wage plus the benefit money. 'The county officials said they'd help us,' says Tony, 'but they didn't do anything, instead they called the Border Patrol on us.'

The strikers also tried, unsuccessfully, to get César Chávez of the United Farmworkers' Union to speak at a rally. By then, that union was a mere shadow of its former self, and Chávez little more than a nationally-known figurehead. By the time of Chávez' death in April 1993, his union held only a handful of contracts and wages had fallen below minimum wage on many of the farms. A new grape boycott was going nowhere, and along with many other contradictions in Chávez' politics - such as joining with the right-wing AFL-CIO and refusing to organise undocumented farm labourers - the UFW was investing union money in highly questionable cheque-cashing outlets. These prey on people with no bank accounts by cashing cheques in return for charges of up to 15 per cent of the cheque amount. The UFW also got involved in building low-cost housing, using non-unionised Mexican workers.

The leaders of the Carpenters Union were merely passive observers of the whole process, happy to have new dues-paying members should this unlikely strike ever succeed. They hadn't organised anyone in years, not even Anglo workers, much less the increasing number of Latinos in the industry.

The city responded to the strike by setting up a special police task force, costing an estimated US$2 million, and the fight began to turn nasty. With 4,000 workers out on strike throughout Southern California, 80 per cent of the construction industry was effectively shut down. The subcontractors put ads in papers looking for strike breakers and plenty showed up, many of them armed. 'At many job sites, we saw all kinds of arms,' says Tony. 'And the police came in and said that they were there to make sure that nobody got injured and to keep the the peace, which is pure bull. They started escorting the scabs from the offices to the job sites.' The drywallers sent a series of flying pickets to the job sites, where they tried to persuade the strike breakers to leave.

Just before the country began to celebrate Independence Day, the Fourth of July, Orange County police arrested 149 strikers *en masse* and threw them into jail for trespassing and suspicion of conspiracy to kidnap. They hit upon the kidnap charge because the strikers had talked six strike breakers into leaving a job site they were picketing. Bail was set at US$50,000 each. The county's medium-security prison was swamped. Extra beds had to be brought in and some two hundred convicted felons were granted emergency sentence reductions on crimes such as assault, burglary and narcotics violations. The Border Patrol found that 88 of the men had no legal documents and began deportation proceedings.

The prosecutor's office realised that they had no hope of making the conspiracy to kidnap charge stick in court and changed the charge to trespassing, a misdemeanour that usually results in a citation and immediate release. Nonetheless, while 47 of the men were released, the rest remained in custody in lieu of bail ranging from US$1,000 to US$10,000. When told that they could plea bargain, pleading guilty in return for a guaranteed release from jail, all 149 men refused. County prosecutors were faced with a long series of trials costing the taxpayers a small fortune. In the end, only 25 of the men were found to be deportable, and the rest of the charges were dropped.

The strike leaders were also charged with racketeering under the so-called Racketeer Influenced and Corrupt Organizations, or RICO act, by which the state must prove continued conspiracy on the part of a group to commit crimes. RICO is usually used to prosecute Mafia members. Although these charges were eventually dropped, Tony believes the police involvement was effective in deterring potential supporters. 'They're scared,' he says of many newly-legalised immigrants. 'They don't want problems with the police and they heard the Border Patrol was checking us. We've told them that it's not true they can be deported for this. They have the constitutional right to go on strike.'

Meanwhile in Orange, San Bernardino, Riverside and Los Angeles counties, the strikers had filed a series of class-action lawsuits in federal court against 200 drywall companies for unfair labour practices. According to their lawyer, Robert Cantore, a statute allows the federal government to stop the sale of products not built in compliance with labour codes, in this case not paying overtime. This would have meant that the developers, with sales already slow because of the recession, would have been prevented from selling their finished homes. By September, companies in every county but San Diego agreed to sign a union contract in return for the suits being dropped.

The striking drywallers had won a partial victory. The majority of them then joined the Carpenters' Union. In San Diego, however, the strikers stayed out. 'The contractors started talking to us,' says Tony, 'we presented our demands to them, they listened and said OK to everything except the union. Here in San Diego,' he notes, 'there are a lot of rich people, a lot of Republicans. They're pro-money and not pro-worker.'

One drywall contractor, Joe Sayatovich, declares that what the strikers were doing was blackmail and against the law. 'We're going to sue them right back for all the damages they have caused us and we'll see if we can't put some of them in jail,' he says. 'We are never going to sign a union contract and let them extort money from us. They're nothing but a bunch of mobsters.'

Although Cantore threatened to bring lawsuits against the companies there as well, by the end of 1992 poverty forced many strikers back to work and the picket lines were taken down.

The story did not end there. The San Diego Drywallers began raising money so the workers could start getting some strike pay again and to revive the picket lines. When the picket lines had come down, those workers lured back to the job sites with higher wages suddenly found them down to rock bottom again. The new members of the Carpenters' Union quickly grew disenchanted with the organisation. They were paying the union about US$200 a month in dues and other charges, according to Tony, and the medical benefits they had been promised failed to materialise. Once again, the men started talking about their own independent union.

❊ ❊ ❊ ❊ ❊

Almost a year later, the charges against strikers are still coming in. Jesús Vásquez, 43, has just come back to the office from a day a court. This time, two strikers have been charged with vandalism and assault. 'But as in all the other cases,' says Jesus, 'this is a lie. The guy who says he got his car windows broken gave a false address and didn't even show up in court.'

Recently, he adds, people have been making citizen's arrests on strikers, who then have to spend two or three days in jail before being freed for lack of evidence. In another case, a security guard accused Tony's work partner, Luciano Salazar, and another striker of firing shots at him. But the picket had been videotaped, proving that the two men had done nothing, and they were freed. As for the current case, says Jesus, 'of course we will win because all of the testimonies, including that of the security guards themselves, show the accusations are false.'

Vásquez is cynical about the authorities' motives, 'It's hard for the police to see that a group of Hispanic Americans and Mexicans are organising. The city of San Diego has done very well out of the construction business. They get a lot of money that way and so they want to protect the industry.' Vásquez points out that the developers are avid donors to political campaign funds during election time.

'I think the most demoralising thing,' he says, 'is to see that people don't understand what's happening to us. We went out on strike because of the low wages, the wages they are paying everyone. Many have gone back because they were promised better wages and conditions. We warned them that they'd take them away again and that's what has happened.'

In the business for 15 years, Jésus Vásquez was born in the state of Jalisco, but grew up in Tijuana. He too used to belong to the union and remembers 'those good years', as he calls them, when he was making up to US$1,200 in a good week. 'My last three children were born when we had medical benefits,' he says, 'so I know what it's like to have all that, paid vacation, dental care and so on. The last two kids were twins and had to spend over a month in an incubator and I didn't have to pay a thing. So it's up to us who once belonged to a union to explain to the others the benefits, the salaries we used to have. I tell the younger guys, who have maybe three or four years experience, about it. They hear this and say, "how is it possible?" But I say it was possible then and if we stick together we can get them again. That's the most important thing, to stick together, to know why we're fighting. The struggle will be hard but we're going to win.'

By 1993 the pickets were out again, and a solidarity committee had been formed in San Diego to help the movement. It included left-wing organisations, Chicano groups and immigrant workers associations. Miguel Caballero, of the California Immigrant Workers Association, or CIWA, says that the strike was a historic event, 'the first time you had this group of Mexican immigrants looking over their economic situation, deciding on their own, without a union, to walk off the job and pull the union and other institutions along with them. It gives a big boost to the people in the labour movement who are arguing for more organising.' Even in Washington, the national director of the AFL-CIO, Joe Shantz, noted that 'throughout the Southwest, it's got workers taking notice of what the drywallers did.'

Tony is optimistic about the final outcome. He is negotiating with the Painters Union, to which the strikers would be able to affiliate as the Independent Union of Drywallers and Tapers of Southern California. 'We want to take the contract away from the Carpenters for misrepresentation,' he explains, 'since they're not doing anything for us anyway. We're going to the National Labour Relations Board in San Diego and then the men will vote.'

'One thing about the Painters,' adds Tony, 'you don't see discrimination there. On their committee, they got women, blacks and Hispanics. And that's the way we feel, we want to represent anyone who will join us.'

Meanwhile he is relieved that nothing more serious has happened over the past year than the arrests and harassment. 'We're lucky with all the noise we've made through the summer that nobody got killed,' he reflects.

❊   ❊   ❊   ❊   ❊

The border, replete with contradictions, geographically and culturally distant from the respective centres of power, defies easy attempts at characterisation. Humid and subtropical at one end, desert-dry and mountainous at the other, it cuts a straight line through two different worlds. One is home. The other is 'the other side'. Yet upon closer scrutiny, the differences begin to melt, revealing a region which is particular unto itself, neither the US nor Mexico.

While there is nowhere in the world quite like it, what is happening on the border reflects the realities of capitalist economies today. Unbridled industrial growth only seems to have unleashed a new series of dichotomies; of poverty amid wealth, of environmental disaster among high-tech factories, of flagrant abuse of people and their rights despite all the talk of democracy and progress. The experiences of the past twenty years or more along the border gives the lie to government and business assertions that uncontrolled economic growth will inevitably improve peoples' lives. New jobs have failed to translate into decent salaries or housing, or into any kind of hope for the future generations of Mexican workers.

Nor, in the end, is the North American Free Trade Agreement anything very new. Business on the border has been squeezing workers for a long time already, and will continue to do so, NAFTA or no NAFTA. Canadian and American workers may not necessarily lose jobs because of increased investment in Mexico, but they will certainly hear threats of moving to

Mexico when they ask for higher wages.

Yet all along the border, people have found ways to get together and demand change, whether it is for water or paved roads in the shanty towns where they are forced to live, or as a short-lived coalition pressing for better wages and work conditions. These are people who believe that change can come, not from presidential decrees or dispassionate analysis, but by people organising and working to change things together, from below. In almost all cases, they have had little help from politicians or unions or American and Canadian social activists. Often, their stories never even become known outside a small circle.

What is perhaps most striking about the issues of *maquiladora* labour and undocumented immigration is the degree to which the US economy has come to depend on them. These two phenomena above all accentuate the most basic problem of lack of democracy. The way Mexican workers on both sides of the border have been continually impeded from fighting back and winning not only respect for their environment and their health, but their labour conditions as well, shows more clearly than ever how the system thrives on depriving workers of their rights.

Which is why there is something both ordinary and extraordinary about people like Petra, or Lupe Torres, or Tony Hernández. Whatever results from them standing up for themselves and their workmates, they have found themselves brushed with a kind of dignity which almost seems out-of-place amid the poverty and lack of opportunity, the absence of learning or history or ideas, that mark their lives. Although their movements are often isolated and small, they will grow as long as there are no answers from their employers and governments. Canadian and American workers, worried about job losses, can help them and themselves if they wake up and start joining forces with them.

Mexico in Brief

Statistics

Area	1,973,000 sq kms
Population	84.8m (1992)
Population Growth Rate	2.1% (1990-92)
Capital	Mexico City (20.2 million, 1990)
Other Cities	Guadalajara (3.2 million, 1990)
	Monterrey (3.0 million, 1990)
Urban Population	74% (1992)

People

Origins	
Mestizo	90.5%
Indigenous	9%
Afro-Mexican	0.5%
Language	Spanish, plus 56 different indigenous language groups
Religion	Roman Catholic 96%

Economy

Gross Domestic Product	$237.7bn (1992)
Per capita GDP	$2,930 (1992)
Real GDP growth	2.7% (ave 1988-93)

GDP by sector (1992)	
Agriculture, Forestry and Fisheries	7.5%
Mining	3.4%
Manufacturing	22.8%
Construction	5.0%
Electricity, gas & water	1.5%
Transport and Communications	6.8%
Commerce, restaurants and hotels	26.1%
Financial services, insurance and real estate	10.7%
Public and private services	17.6%
Less imputed banking services	-1.4%
Total	100%

Exports (1993) $29.4bn
Imports (1993) $48.9bn
Trade balance (1993)   -$19.5bn
Current account (1993)   -$21.0bn

Principal exports: Manufactured goods (51.3%); petroleum (26.1%); Value added on *maquiladora*-produced goods (13.2%); agriculture, forestry and fisheries (7.6%)

Principal imports: Manufactured goods (92.9%); agriculture, forestry and fisheries (5.5%)

Main trading partners (1991)
exports to: US (74.5%); EC (8.6%); Canada (5.5%); Japan (4.1%)
imports from: US (70.7%); EC (12.6%); Japan (6.0%); Canada (0.8%)

Total external debt	$125bn (1993)
Per capita debt	$1,474 (1993)
Debt service as % of exports of goods and services (1993)	17%
Inflation	8.7% (1993)
Exchange rate peso/US dollar	3.34 (March 1994)

Society

Housing	deficit of over 6 million homes, 40% of existing homes substandard
Life expectancy	69 (1991)
Infant mortality per thousand live births	36 (1990)
No access to health facilities	15% (1985-88)
No access to safe water	11% (1985-88)
Rural population with no access to safe water	53%
Adult literacy rate male	90% (1990)
female	85% (1990)

Extreme malnutrition	8% (1974); 15% (1989)
Rural children malnourished	50%
Per capita milk consumption	125 litres (1980); 74 litres (1990)
Average calorie intake per day	1,653 calories (1987); 1,431 calories (1990)
Rural homes under poverty line	43%
Urban homes under poverty line	23%
Unemployment	18% (1990)

Sources: Tom Barry, *Mexico: A Country Guide*, 1992; Economist Intelligence Unit; Europa Publications, *South America, Central America and the Caribbean, 1991*; Inter-American Development Bank; Latin America Monitor; National Indigenous Institute; Organisation for Economic Co-operation and Development; UN Department of International Economic and Social Affairs; UN Development Programme; UN Economic Commission for Latin America and the Caribbean.

Acronyms

AFL-CIO	American Federation of Labor-Congress of Industrial Organizations
AFSC	American Friends Service Committee
CANACINTRA	*Cámara Nacional de la Industria de la Transformación* National Chamber of Manufacturing Industry
CCPM	*Comité Cívico Popular Mixteco* Mixtec Popular Civic Committee
CDP	*Comité de Defensa Popular* Peoples' Defence Committee
CIWA	California Immigrant Workers Association
CROC	*Confederación Revolucionaria de Obreros y Campesinos* Revolutionary Confederation of Workers and Campesinos
CROM	*Confederación Regional Obrera Mexicana* Regional Mexican Workers Confederation
CTM	*Confederación de Trabajadores de México* Mexican Workers Confederation
ECLAC	UN Economic Commission for Latin America and the Caribbean
EPA	Environmental Protection Agency
FAIR	Federation for American Immigration Reform
GATT	General Agreement on Tariffs and Trade
IMSS	*Instituto Mexicano de Seguro Social* Mexican Institute of Social Security
INEA	*Instituto Nacional de Educación para Adultos* National Institute of Adult Education
INEGI	*Instituto Nacional de Estadística, Geografía e Informática* National Institute of Geography and Statistics
INFONAVIT	*Instituto del Fondo Nacional de la Vivienda para los Trabajadores* National Institute for Workers' Housing

INS   Immigration and Naturalization Service

IRCA   Immigration Reform and Control Act

OIG   Office of the Inspector General

PAN   *Partido de Acción Nacional*
           National Action Party

PARM   *Partido Auténtico de la Revolución Mexicana*
           Authentic Party of the Mexican Revolution

PEMEX   *Petroleós Mexicanos*
           state oil company

PRI   *Partido Revolucionario Institucional*
           Institutional Revolutionary Party

PRONAF   *Programa Nacional Fronterizo*
           National Border Program

PT   *Partido de Trabajo*
           Labour Party

RICO   Racketeer Influenced and Corrupt Organizations

SECOFI   *Secretaría de Comercio y Fomento Industrial*
           Mexican Trade Secretariat

SEDESOL   *Secretaría de Desarrollo Social*
           federal environment agency (successor to SEDUE)

SEDUE   *Secretaría de Desarrollo Urbano y Ecologia*
           federal environment agency

SJOI   *Sindicato de Jornaleros y Obreros Industriales*
           Union of Dayworkers and Industrial Workers

UFW   United Farmworkers

Further Reading

Maquiladoras

General

Baker, Stephen, 'Detroit South', *Business Week*, March 16, 1992

Barry, Tom (ed), *Mexico: A Country Guide*, Hemispheric Resource Center, Albuquerque, New Mexico, 1992

Langewieshe, William, 'The Border', *The Atlantic*, 2-part series, May & June, 1992

Martínez, Oscar J., *Border Boom Town: Ciudad Juárez Since 1848*, University of Texas Press, Austin and London, 1975

Martínez, Oscar J., *Troublesome Border*, University of Arizona Press, Tucson

Nathan, Debbie, *Women and Other Aliens: Essays from the US-Mexican Border*, Cinco Puntos Press, El Paso, Texas, 1991

Secretaría de Comercio y Fomento Industrial, *La Industria Maquiladora de Exportación y El Tratado de Libre Comercio*, Mexico City, 1991

Secretaría de Comercio y Fomento Industrial, *Directorio Nacional de la Industria Maquiladora de Exportación*, Mexico City, 1992

Shaiken, Harley, *Mexico and the Global Economy: High Technology and Work Organization in Export Industries*, Center for US-Mexican Studies, University of California, San Diego, 1990

Shorris, Earl, 'Borderline Cases', *Harper's Magazine*, August 1990

Sklair, Leslie, *Assembling for Development: The Maquila Industry in Mexico and the United States*, Center for US-Mexico Studies, University of California, San Diego, 1993

Labour

Anguiano, Arturo, 'El Estado y La Política Obrera del Cardenismo', *Editorial Era*, Mexico City, 11th edition, 1990

Frontera Norte, 'Condiciones y Vida de los Trabajadores de la Maquiladora en Tijuana y Nogales,' Vol. 2, # 4, July-Dec., 1990, Tijuana, B.C.

Iglesias, Norma, 'La Flor Más Bella de la Maquiladora,' Secretaría de Educación Pública, Mexico City, 1985

Quintero Ramírez, Cirila, 'La Sindicalización en las Maquiladoras Tijuanenses, 1970 - 1988', Consejo Nacional para la Cultura y las Artes, Mexico City, 1990

Quintero Ramírez, Cirila, 'Sindicalismo Tradicional en las Maquiladoras, El Caso de Matamoros,' paper given at the Second Nuevo Laredo Symposium on Border Problems, Sept. 1991

Quintero Ramírez, Cirila, 'Reestructuración Sindical y la Mujer Trabajadora en las Maquiladoras Fronterizas,' paper given at the Segunda Semana de la Mujer, Matamoros, Tamps., March 1992

Health and the Environment

Coalition for Justice in the Maquiladoras, *Maquiladoras: A Broken Promise*, AFL - CIO publication number 0227-0491-1, Washington, D.C.

Denman, Catalina A., 'La Salud de las Obreras de la Maquila: El Caso de Nogales, Sonora,' published in *Crisis, Conflicto y Sobrevivencia: Estudio Sobre la Sociedad Urbana en México*, Universidad de Guadalajara, Guadalajara, 1990

Denman, Catalina A., 'Productos Tóxicos y Potencialmente Peligrosos en la Industria Fronteriza,' published in *Ecología y Recursos Naturales y Medio Ambiente en Sonora*, Colegio de Sonora/ Gobierno del Estado de Sonora, Hermosillo, 1992

Kochan, Leslie, *The Maquiladoras and Toxics: The Hidden Costs of Production South of the Border*, Leslie Kochan, AFL - CIO Publication No. 186, Feb. 1989

Perry, Diane M., Roberto Sánchez, William H. Glaze, Marisa Mazari, 'Binational Management of Hazardous Waste: The Maquiladora Industry at the US-Mexican Border', *Environmental Management*, Vol 14, No. 4, Los Angeles, 1990

Satchell, Michael, 'Poisoning the Border', *US News & World Report*, 6 May 1991

Texas Department of Health, *An Investigation of a Cluster of Neural Tube Defects in Cameron County, Texas*, Austin, 1992

Immigration

Americas Watch, 'Brutality Unchecked: Human Rights Abuses Along the US Border with Mexico', May 1992

Bustamante, Jorge A., *Measuring the Flow of Undocumented Immigrants: Research Findings from the Zapata Canyon Project*, El Colegio de la Frontera Norte, Tijuana, 1990

Cornelius, Wayne and Bustamante, Jorge A. (eds), *Mexican Migration to the United States: Origins, Consequences, and Policy Options*, Center for US- Mexican Studies, University of California, San Diego, 1989

Cornelius, Wayne, 'Impacts of Free Trade on Mexican Labor Migration', paper given at the Symposium on North American Free Trade, San Diego May 1991

Cornelius, Wayne, 'Impacts of the 1986 US Immigration Law on Emigration from Rural Mexican Sending Communities', in *Undocumented Migration to the United States: IRCA and the Experience of the 1980s*, Frank D. Bean, Barry Edmonston, and Jeffrey Passel, eds, The Urban Institute Press, Washington, D.C., 1990

Davidson, Miriam, 'The Mexican Border War', *The Nation*, 12 Nov. 1990

Greenwood, Michael J., *The Labor Market Consequences of US Immigration: A Survey*, Center for Economic Analysis, University of Colorado at Boulder and John M. McDowell, Department of Economics, Arizona State University

Sassen, Saskia, *The Mobility of Labour and Capital: A Study in International Investment and Labour Flow*, Cambridge University Press, Cambridge, 1988

Second Report of the Immigration Law Enforcement Monitoring Project, 'Human Rights at the Mexico-US Border', AFSC, Philadelphia, March, 1990

Shorris, Earl, 'Raids, Racism and the INS', Earl Shorris, *The Nation*, May 8, 1989

Third Report of the Immigration Law Enforcement Monitoring Project, 'Sealing Our Borders: The Human Toll', AFSC, Philadelphia, Feb. 1992

Resources and Action

Details about organisations in the US, Canada and Mexico are drawn from *Cross-Border Links*, published by the Inter-Hemispheric Resource Center (see below - United States).

UK and Ireland

CAFOD
2 Romero Close
Stockwell Road
London
SW9 9TY
Tel 071 733 7900
Fax 071 274 9630

Supports a small number of development projects in Mexico working on issues such as popular education and sustainable development. CAFOD also supports Mexican organisations involved in education and information work.

Mexico Solidarity Group
c/o CAHRC
83 Margaret Street
London
W1N 7HB

Organises workshops and seminars, and produces a quarterly newsletter, in support of the Mexican people in their struggle for justice.

Oxfam
274 Banbury Road
Oxford
OX2 7DZ
Tel 0865 311311

Has a small programme in Mexico focusing on urban issues, research on the effects of NAFTA, and indigenous people in the south of the country.

Trócaire
169 Booterstown Avenue
Blackrock
Co Dublin
Ireland

Tel 010 353 1 288 5385
Fax 010 353 1 288 3577

Has information on education and campaigning work in Ireland on Latin American-US relations.

Womankind Worldwide
122 Whitechapel High Street
London E1 7PT
Tel: 071 247 6931
Fax: 071 247 3436

Supports women's own initiatives in developing countries to get training and education, credit, better health, freedom from violence and to improve their organisational effectiveness. In the UK, Womankind raises awareness of women's concerns and their contributions to their communities. In Mexico, Womankind supports small one-off initiatives ranging from producing manuals for activists and popular educators, to a community workshop on making solar ovens in Oaxaca, to a peasant women's conference in Guadalajara relecting on indigenous women's experiences over the 500 years.

Canada

Coalition québécoise sur les négociations trilatérales
1601 Rue de Lorimier
Montreal, PQ H2K 4M5
Tel: 514 598 2273
Fax: 514 598 2052

Clearing house for information from Quebec-based organisations on the impact of NAFTA.

Common Frontiers
11 Madison Avenue
Toronto, ON M5R 2S2
Tel: 416 961 7847
Fax: 416 924 5356
Email: (WEB) comfront

Coalition of groups monitoring NAFTA and the Enterprise for the Americas initiative. Promotes trilateral links between popular organisations, through its Mexican office and contacts in the US and Canada.

Ecumenical Coalition for Economic Justice
11 Madison Ave
Toronto, ON M5R 2S2
Tel: 416 921 4615
Fax: 416 924 5356

Engages in research, education and political action on global issues of economic justice. Current priorities include NAFTA and women's work. Publishes quarterly *Economic Justice Report*.

Mujer a Mujer
606 Shaw St
Toronto, ON M6G 3L6
Tel: 416 532 8584
Email: (WEB) perg

See entry under US for details.

Mexico

Fronteras Comunes
Centro Coordinador de Proyectos Ecuménicos (CECOPE)
Río Niágara 40 bis
Col Cuauhtémoc
México D.F. 06500
Tel: 5 511 1781
Fax: 5 511 1781
Email: (PeaceNet) cecope

See entry under Canada for details.

Mujer a Mujer
AP 24-553
Col Roma
México, D.F. 06701
Tel: 5 207 0834
Fax: 5 584 1068
Email: (PeaceNet) igc:mam

See entry under US for details.

Red Mexicana de Acción Frente al Libre Comercio (RMALC)
Godard 20
Col. Guadalupe Victoria
México, D.F. 07790
Tel: 5 556 9375/14
Fax: 5 556 9316
Email: (PeaceNet) igc:rmalc

Network of labour, peasant, women's and environmental organisations aiming to
raise awareness on social and other costs of NAFTA. Publishes monthly bulletin,
Alternativas, and other material.

United States

American Friends Service Committee
1501 Cherry St
Philadelphia, PA 19102
Tel: 215 241 7132
Fax: 215 241 7275

An organisation of US Quakers. Runs a US-Mexico Border Program, Maquiladora
Project, Immigration Law Enforcement Monitoring Project (ILEMP) and Women
and Global Corporations Project. Works on issues related to illegal migrants, the
social and environmental impact of the *maquiladora* industry and promotes
cooperation between US and Mexican organisations affected by NAFTA. Publishes
reports and other resources.

Border Ecology Project
PO Box 5
Naco, AZ 85620
Tel: 602 432 7456
Fax: 602 432 7456

Organisation of residents and environmental organisations on both sides of the
border campaigning on issues including air quality, water management and toxic
waste. Publishes *Directory of Ecology in the Border Region* and other materials.

Coalition for Justice in the Maquiladoras
530 Bandera Rd
San Antonio
Texas, TX 78228
Tel: 512 735 4988
Fax: 512 735 2615

A US-Mexican coalition of religious, environmental, labour, Latino and women's organisations seeking to pressure US transnational corporations to adopt socially responsible practices within the *maquiladora* industry. Publishes newsletter and other materials.

Development Gap for Alternative Policies
1400 I St. NW #520
Washington, DC 20005
Tel: 202 898 1566
Fax: 202 898 1612
Email: (PeaceNet) cdp!dgap

Lobby group seeking to inject local perspectives from the countries of the South into policy-making circles in the North. Focuses on economic issues including structural adjustment, aid and trade. Publishes bimonthly newsletter, *Naftathoughts*, and other resources.

Inter-Hemispheric Education Resource Center
PO Box 4506
Albuquerque, NM 87196-4506
Tel: 505 842 8288
Fax: 505 246 1601
Email: (PeaceNet) resourcectr

Produces books, policy reports and audiovisuals on Mexico, Central America and the Caribbean on issues such as US aid, low-intensity conflict, land and hunger, and the role of private US organisations and churches.

Mujer a Mujer
PO Box 12322
San Antonio
Texas, TX 78212

Organises exchanges, workshops, tours and activist retreats to promote strategic cooperation among grassroots and feminist organisations in Mexico, Canada and the US. See other sections for Canadian and Mexican offices. Publishes *Correspondencia*, quarterly English and Spanish newsletter

Index

O

Oaxaca   85, 86, 90, 91, 96, 97
Obregón, President Alvaro   34
off-shore manufacturing   6, 17, 89
Operation Wetback   118

P

Packard Electric   42, 43
PAN   27
Parker Hannifin O-Ring   59, 60, 71
PARM   35
PEMEX   10, 15, 34, 38, 62, 106
Phillips   21
Phoenix   120
pollution   54, 55, 56, 57, 58, 59, 61,
    63, 65
Porfirio Díaz, President   20
pregnancy   1, 2, 13, 52, 53, 66, 68,
    72, 83, 112, 122
Preservation Products   49, 51, 70
PRI   7, 11, 15, 27, 34, 35, 47, 54,
    55, 56, 121
PRONAF   15, 23
PT   27

Q

Química Fluor   62, 63, 64
Química Orgánica   51, 52

R

racism   80, 82, 83, 94-98, 113, 117,
    118, 121
rape   29, 78, 79, 82, 83, 84, 92, 114,
    125
Reagan, President Ronald   95, 123
Retzloff   49, 50, 51, 64
Reynosa   1, 2, 3, 5, 8, 13, 19, 38, 39,
    40, 52, 54, 60, 62, 68, 69, 70, 71,
    106, 107
RICO   126
Rio Grande   3, 6, 16, 20, 29, 31, 53,
    56, 59, 64, 72, 104, 108, 111
RSR-Quemetco   61

S

sackings   22, 39, 40
Salinas de Gortari, President Carlos
    9, 10, 11, 12, 55, 61, 62, 64
Samsonite   74
San Antonio   78, 106
San Diego   6, 30, 47, 79, 80, 81, 82,
    83, 84, 91, 92, 94, 95, 96, 98, 99,
    107, 108, 110, 111, 113, 116, 117,
    118, 123, 124, 125, 127, 128, 129
schools   5, 24, 27, 28, 29, 32, 40,
    60, 61, 66, 67, 68, 75, 77, 97,
    106, 108, 110, 114, 117, 118
SECOFI   6, 17
SEDESOL   51, 54, 55, 60, 61, 62
SEDUE   51, 52, 54, 59, 60, 63
service industries   7, 87
sexual harassment   5, 45, 114, 116
shanty towns   3, 78, 90, 130
SIDERMEX   10
Sinopac International   13
SJOI   33, 35, 37
social security   87
Solidev Mexicana   45
Solitron Devices   45, 47
Sonora   22, 28, 58, 59, 70, 74, 83,
    103
South Korea   8, 9
Soviet Union   9, 94
Stepan   49, 51
strikes   28, 29, 31, 34, 35, 36, 38,
    39, 40, 41, 42, 44, 46, 47, 71, 77,
    104, 123, 126, 127, 128

T

Taiwan   8, 9, 17
Tamaulipas   31, 54, 55
Tampico   37
tax   6, 9, 19, 20, 36, 61, 89, 95
Texas   3, 4, 6, 19, 20, 25, 30, 31, 32,
    37, 53, 54, 55, 59, 72, 78, 104,
    108, 109, 111, 112, 113, 116, 117,
    118
Texas Rangers   108, 109, 118
textiles   18, 19, 28, 70

Latin America Bureau Books

For Richer, For Poorer
Shaping US-Mexican Integration
by Harry Browne

Whatever the future of the North American Free Trade Agreement (NAFTA), the US and Mexico are involved in a rapid and unstoppable process of economic integration. Driven by the changing global production systems of US and other transnational corporations, the two countries' economies are now more closely intertwined then ever before.

But NAFTA, with its business-first brand of integration, has been criticised as little more than a corporate bill of rights, allowing big corporations to take advantage of cheap labour and lax environmental regulation in Mexico, and to play one labour movement off against another. NAFTA has provoked an unprecedented level of public interest and criticism from a unique coalition of environmentalists, trade unionists and human rights activists.

For Richer, For Poorer explains the nuts and bolts of globalisation, and explores the winners and losers in NAFTA-style free trade. It examines who opposes and supports NAFTA in the US and Mexico and looks at their arguments. The book outlines alternative strategies to promote a more balanced process of integration that protects workers' rights and the environment as well as business interests.

Harry Browne is co-author of *The Great Divide: The Challenges of US-Mexico Relations in the 1990s* (Grove Atlantic, 1994) and *Runaway America: US Jobs and Factories on the Move* (Resource Center Press, 1993). He is a research associate at the Inter-Hemispheric Education Resource Center in Albuquerque, New Mexico.

128pp with index   ISBN 0 906156 90 4   Price £8.80

US orders: $9.95 plus $3 postage from:
The Resource Center, Box 4506, Albuquerque, NM 87196, USA

Mexico: A Country Guide
Tom Barry (ed)

'By far the best first stop for factual analysis... Almost everything imaginable is covered in great detail, and there are strong sections on women's and social movements.'
New Internationalist magazine

What is the human rights situation in Mexico? Is there a strong women's movement? What is the future of the political opposition? How will the free trade agreement affect jobs? Who's who in the business community? What are the major environmental issues? How healthy is the popular movement? How important is US aid and investment?

Mexico: A Country Guide addresses these and many other issues for all readers wanting to understand the forces shaping Mexico today.

Tom Barry is principal writer and analyst at the Resource Center in Albuquerque, New Mexico.

300 pages with photos and diagrams   ISBN 0-911213-36   £10.90

US orders: $9.95 plus $3 postage from:
The Resource Center, Box 4506, Albuquerque, NM 87196, USA

The Latin American City
Alan Gilbert

Since the 1950s, Latin America has been transformed from a rural to an urban society. The region now contains some of the world's biggest cities, headed by Mexico City with its 20 million inhabitants. In all but five Latin American countries, more people now live in towns and cities than in the countryside.

This mass movement from country to city has put enormous strain on the infrastructure and services of cities such as Bogotá and Caracas. Conditions continue to worsen as governments cut back social spending in their structural adjustment programmes.

The Latin American City looks at the region's urban explosion from the perspective of the poor. It asks why people are attracted to the city and examines the underlying problem of rural poverty which fuels the exodus. It explores the options open to those arriving in the city and the strategies used in order to acquire land and build a home. Highlighting the role of the informal sector in urban survival, it also explains how popular organisation and protest can result in improved living standards for the poor.

'Alan Gilbert has long been one of the most incisive and perceptive analysts of urban problems and policy in Latin America. **The Latin American City** should

be extremely useful in interdisciplinary survey courses on contemporary Latin America as well as courses dealing comparatively with cities in Third World countries. Gilbert's coverage of urban issue areas ... is the most comprehensive of any text to date.'
Professor Wayne A. Cornelius, University of California.

Alan Gilbert is Professor of Geography at University College, London. He is the author of many books on Latin American development issues and urbanisation, including *Latin America* (Routledge, 1990) and *Latin American Development* (Pelican, 1974).

| 190pp | ISBN 0 906156 82 3 (pbk) | £9.90 |
| $17.00 | ISBN 0 906156 83 1(hbk) | £19.90 |

Compañeras
Voices from the Latin American women's movement
Edited by Gaby Küppers

'Feminism' first appeared in Latin American popular vocabulary as a term of abuse reserved for foreign 'man-haters'. **Compañeras: the Latin American Women's Movement** shows that twenty years later, it has become a topic for serious debate amongst wide sectors of Latin American society.

The change in attitudes stems from an upsurge in women's activism throughout the continent over the past decade. Diversity is the hallmark of this activism, reflected in the 25 interviews and essays by Latin American women activists in **Compañeras**. Contributors range from a Mexican prostitute who recently stood for parliament and a group of Colombian steelworkers' wives to Nicaraguan feminist, Sofia Montenegro, and members of the Brazilian PT.

'In the bars of Cochabamba today, you often hear men say, 'well, as far as I'm concerned, I'm no machista.' They've heard the term, 'machista' from their wives as something negative..so feminism has managed to penetrate the public consciousness.'
Jael Bueno, Bolivian feminist

| 192 pages with index | ISBN 0 906156 86 6 (pbk) | £9.90 |
| $17.00 | | |

Prices are for paperback editions and include postage and packing.

LAB Books are available by post from Latin America Bureau, 1 Amwell Street, London EC1R 1UL. Cheques payable to LAB. Write for a free catalogue.

US$ orders for LAB books should be sent to Monthly Review Press, 122 West 27th Street, New York, NY 10001. Cheques payable to Monthly Review Press.

VICTIMS OF DEVELOPMENT
Resistance and Alternatives
JEREMY SEABROOK

Jeremy Seabrook is one of England's most imaginative and creative writers, with a preacher's talent for prophecy and a capacity for righteous indignation reminiscent of George Orwell. *Victims of Development*, his latest collection of political essays, carries forward an argument that the concept of 'development', as conceived of in the First World, has proved to be a disastrous doctrine that brings death and destruction in its wake... The key to understanding where we might (or should) be going is to examine where we are. And here Seabrook is an enlightened, almost a visionary, guide.
Richard Gott, *The Guardian*

256 pages, 1993
Paperback ISBN 086091 611 1
Hardback ISBN 086091 385 6

THE PACIFICATION OF CENTRAL AMERICA
Political Change in the Isthmus, 1987–1993
JAMES DUNKERLEY

This unique guide to the labyrinthine politics of Central America opens with a succinct overview of pacification and democracy in the region. The first section comprises an analytical essay focusing on the causes and consequences of the ending of civil war in El Salvador, Guatemala and Nicaragua. The second section consists of a detailed chronology covering all key developments between 1987 and 1993. The book concludes with an indispensable series of appendices which clearly set out statistical profiles of Costa Rica, El Salvador, Guatemala, Honduras and Nicaragua for the decade since 1982.

168 pages, 1994
Paperback ISBN 086091 648 0
Hardback ISBN 086091 423 2

VERSO

For further information about books available from Verso please write to:
USA: 29 West 35th Street, New York, NY 10001-2291
UK & Rest of World: 6 Meard Street, London W1V 3HR